Business Income
Insurance Demystified

Business Income Insurance Demystified

The Simplified Guide to Time Element Coverages

Christopher J. Boggs

CPCU, ARM, ALCM, LPCS, AAI, APA, CWCA, CRIS, AINS

Contents

Chapter 1
Business Income's Importance

Few insurance products elicit as much fear or visceral reactions as business income protection (a.k.a. time element coverage). Without being overly glib, business income concepts are actually simple to understand and explain. The reason such "fear" exists is because the coverage has long been shrouded in mystery and taught incorrectly by instructors who themselves do not completely understand the coverage.

Grasping and properly applying business income coverage requires little more than an understanding of time; because business income is almost entirely based on time. The amount of business income coverage and the coinsurance calculation are almost of secondary importance. In fact, determining the correct coinsurance percentage and coverage limit is the direct result of accurately estimating the time necessary for a business to return to full operational capability. And, contrary to popular belief, an intimate understanding of financial documents (income statements, balance sheets, etc.) is **not** necessary to construct a proper business income program.

Business Income's Necessity

According to Federal Emergency Management Agency (FEMA) U.S. Fire Administration statistics, 103,500 non-residential and commercial structure fires occurred in the

United States during 2009. This equates to a non-residential or commercial structure being damaged by fire every five minutes. Those 103,500 fires resulted in nearly $3.1 billion in direct property damage alone; not reported is the indirect business income loss amount. (Remember, a business income loss is considered an indirect loss that results from a direct loss such as fire).

Tracking down accurate statistical data on the number of businesses that never reopen after a catastrophic property loss, such as one caused by fire, is difficult and bordering on impossible. The insurance industry has long stated that 25% of the businesses that suffer a catastrophic loss (defined as one causing a total shut down of 30 days or more) never reopen. The percentage could actually be much higher.

Not included in this often-quoted statistic is the percentage of the businesses that do reopen but ultimately close within a short time (within three to five years) of the catastrophic loss, with such failure being directly traceable and attributable to the catastrophic loss. Considering these "long-tail" business closures, the failure rate due directly to catastrophic loss could approach 45 or 50%.

Further, data from the Institute for Business & Home Safety (www.ibhs.org) states that 25% of businesses that close for a long period due to a "major disaster" never reopen. This differs from the previous statistic as this data contemplates only businesses closed by a "major disaster." A "major disaster" is a communal event (i.e. a hurricane or flood) rather than an individual event like fire. Thus, 25% of businesses closed due to a hurricane (for example) never reopen; and this data doesn't contemplate Hurricane Katrina.

Individually "catastrophic" losses and "major disaster" (communal) losses combine to result in the closure of thousands of businesses in any given year. If 60% of all non-residential and commercial fires qualify as "catastrophic" (some reports indicate as high as 90%), then America lost approximately 15,525 businesses (employers) in 2010. Add the "catastrophic" loss closures to the statistically developed "major disaster" business closures reported by IBHS, and the number of business failures due to both individual and communal disasters in 2009 could ultimately top 25,000.

What It Means

Most businesses that never reopen or close after reopening as a direct result of an individual catastrophe or community disaster don't close because of the lack of building and business personal property coverage; they close because there is no money coming in the door. Few businesses can remain viable without a source of income. Mortgages have to be paid, rental expenses continue (building, machinery, and equipment rentals), employees want to get paid (or they find other jobs), and the insurance carrier wants its premium. These and other expenses continue even if the business is not open.

Businesses don't own buildings, machinery, and equipment for the pride of ownership. Property, plant, and equipment serve a purpose; to make money. If they don't make money, they are of little use to the business; other than as an expense. Even buildings constructed to impress people and draw them in (like the casinos in Las Vegas) are intended to draw people in to spend money. Profit is the motive, and business income coverage insures and protects that motivation.

In short, business income coverage may be the most important protection any business purchases. It is certainly the most important property coverage. A business that is shut down for six months due to a major property loss could be fully insured for the building damage and even the contents, but still be unable to reopen (or ultimately fail) because no money is flowing in to pay all the continuing, non-loss-related expenses. Conversely, the building and equipment could be horribly underinsured, but if there is business income coverage, the business could still reopen and even succeed. Getting a loan to make up the difference between the insurance proceeds and the actual cost to rebuild is much easier when the business can show the bank that there is enough money coming in the door to keep the business afloat while repairs are being made.

Obviously, the optimal goal is to have the building, contents, and business income all properly insured; but of the three, the most important is business income.

You Have 2 Minutes to Explain Business Income

U.S. and European studies seem to jointly conclude that the average adult attention span is somewhere between 10 and 20 minutes. Of course, attention spans vary among individuals and is shortened or lengthened by such factors as the listener's:

- Interest in the topic
- Knowledge of the topic (or desire to learn more)
- Feelings toward the person talking and the relationship
- External business or personal issues and problems
- Health
- Length of their "To Do" list

This means that when an agent or broker meets with an insured or prospect, he or she has only 20 and maybe up to 30 minutes to address all the necessary insurance issues before the insured is no longer hearing or retaining what is said. Many topics must be tackled in that short time span; some are a re-hashing of mundane and common information, but some time has to be invested in new topics, coverage issues, and coverage gaps.

Business income is one coverage topic that requires attention. But because of everything else that must be covered in any given meeting, agents have about two minutes to introduce business income protection and move the insured towards more interest and desire in the coverage.

The average person, speaking at a normal pace with necessary emphasis and inflection, speaks between 200 and 225 words per minute. This means that the business income concept and "buy-in" must be delivered in approximately 400 words to fall within the two-minute window.

Following is a script that can be customized to model each agent's style, but it delivers the message in about two minutes. Don't believe it, get a stop watch, speak normally and read the script out loud.

Ready...GO!

"Your business exists to make money; money to pay your employees, cover the business' bills (such as rent/mortgage, supplies, taxes, and so on) and hopefully enough money for your personal use and benefit. The money you take home pays for your necessities (a house, food, clothes, etc.) and especially those 'niceties' like a bigger house, great vacations, private school, etc.

Without an income stream, employees don't get paid, bills don't get paid, and YOU don't get paid. And with no income or source of surplus capital, your employees will find other jobs, bills will go unpaid, and your personal financial situation will suffer.

Business income protection assures that your business and you maintain a stream of income following a major loss.

Estimates are that 25% of all businesses suffering a 'catastrophic loss,' one that causes them to close for more than 30 days, never reopen. And about another 25% close within three to five years following the loss. We can't find credible information on the effect of these closures on the business owner's personal financial picture.

It is highly unlikely that these businesses closed due to the lack of or improperly written or valued insurance on the building or the contents. Generally, these businesses closed due simply to the lack of INCOME. You may be able to get a loan to aid in rebuilding the building or replacing the contents; but lost income is just that – lost.

Yes, there is an additional premium to cover your business income. But rather than an expense, this coverage must be viewed as an investment in the continued viability of your company. Of all the property coverages available, this is the most important. Without a flow of income or massive cash reserves, your business may cease to exist, along with your personal income, following a major loss.

Business income coverage is actually exceptionally cheap protection considering the alternative. Does this sound like protection you could use?"

STOP! About 10 or 15 seconds should be left in the two-minute window. If the insured's interest in or desire for business income protection is piqued, there should be some follow up questions like:

- How much is the coverage going to cost? (Almost always a question.)
- How much information do you need and when do you need it?
- What information do you need?
- Can my accountant provide the necessary information?

Granted, these are not all the questions that may be asked, only a sampling. But questions are great because that means the agent has permission to extend the conversation and the insured has reengaged the meeting.

Of course, the answers to the above questions (and any others asked) depend on many factors such as limits, rates, coverage options chosen, and the insured's willingness to provide the necessary information. With the help of this book, answering these questions is easy.

This Book

<u>Business Income Insurance Demystified</u> details all aspects of business income coverage from the worksheet through the completion of the business income application. With this information, the historical (or hysterical) fear surrounding business income insurance should disappear.

Chapter 2
Four Key Business Income Concepts

Business income protection is of utmost importance for any insured suffering a catastrophic property loss. To fully understand business income coverage and the protection the policy extends, four key business income definitions and concepts must be covered up front:

- Business income
- Period of restoration
- Operational capability
- Time doctrine

Each of these definitions and concepts is referenced throughout this book. Understanding these terms and theories from the beginning allows a better understanding of the business income policy specifics detailed in the remainder of this book.

Business Income

Business income (BI) is partially defined in both available coverage forms (CP 00 30 and CP 00 32) as: "*Net income... that would have been earned or incurred and [PLUS] continuing normal operating expense incurred, including payroll.*" Two key terms in this definition require a more in-depth analysis: 1) "net income;" and 2) "continuing normal operating expenses."

Net Income: Net income as used in the business income form is not defined the same as it is in the world of finance; this is why the business income report/worksheet (CP 15 15), detailed in Chapter 4, cannot simply be handed to the insured or its accountant without explanation. In the context of business income, "net income" means the entity's net profit (or loss) before the application of income taxes. In practicality, the BI meaning of net income can be best explained to the accountant as real and potential earnings before taxes (EBT).

How does this definition differ from the financial world's definition of "net income?" In finance and accounting, net income is understood to mean, "Gross revenue minus all business and production-related expenses." In finance and accounting, net income only deals with and accounts for money actually earned; in business income, potential income is contemplated in the coverage (detailed more fully in Chapter 4).

Notice also that in business income coverage net income includes "net loss." Why would a business operating at a loss require business income protection? Simple; a business-closing loss would likely create a greater net loss than would have been incurred had no loss occurred. For example, a business that would have experienced a $100,000 net loss had nothing occurred instead suffers a $500,000 net loss because of a direct property loss. Business income coverage would pay the $400,000 difference to indemnify the insured and put them in the same financial condition that would have existed had no loss occurred.

Continuing Normal Operating Expenses:
Continuing normal operating expenses are those normal operating expenditures that continue, in whole or in part, during the time the business operations are shut down or reduced due to a direct property loss (the "Period of Restoration"). These expenses can include mortgage/rent, insurance, payroll (unless altered by an endorsement), and various others. Prior to the loss, the insured is not charged with knowing which expenses will continue, which will be reduced, and which will disappear completely following a loss.

Business income losses are calculated by adding the net income that potentially WOULD have been earned had no loss occurred to the usual and customary operating expenses that continue during the period of restoration. So, the BI calculation requires adding an estimation (of the possible net income) to an actualization (continuing normal operating expenses incurred during the period of restoration). Business income's loss determination is more specifically explored in Chapter 3 (see the subhead "Loss Determination").

Period of Restoration

Business income's period of restoration is the time period beginning a specific amount of time following the direct physical loss or damage to the insured structure (usually 72 hours, but the time can be lowered by endorsement) and ending on the earlier of: the date the property should be repaired, rebuilt, or replaced with reasonable speed and similar quality; or the date when operations are resumed at a new permanent location.

During the period of restoration, several objectives must be accomplished to assure the operation can return to operational capability as quickly as possible. The importance and depth of the concept of the period of restoration to business income requires a separate chapter. Chapter 5 details the specifics of business income's period of restoration.

Operational Capability

Operational capability is a non-policy business income term describing the end of the period of restoration. This is the point at which a manufacturing operation can return to pre-loss production and inventory levels (excluding the time necessary to produce the same amount of finished stock on hand prior to the loss) or a non-manufacturing entity can operate with the same level of inventory, equipment, and efficiency as before the operation-closing loss. Operational capability is accomplished either by repairing or rebuilding the current location, or by finding a new permanent location.

To clarify, operational capability is not synonymous with a return to pre-loss income levels, which may take much longer to accomplish (see Extended Business Income details in Chapter 8). Operational capability is merely the entity's ability to produce goods and provide services at the same level, efficiency, and speed as they did before the loss (the ability to conduct operations at pre-loss levels).

Time Doctrine

A "doctrine" is a principle or body of principles; the time doctrine is the principle around which business income coverage is based. The doctrine is not found in the policy or any other literature detailing business income coverage. It is unique to this book.

Business income exists to insure the continued financial viability of the insured's business by replacing the net income that would have been earned had no loss occurred and pay any usual and customary expenses that continue during the period of restoration (the period when the insured is non-operational or operating at a reduced capacity) indemnifying the insured. To that end, we have defined the time doctrine as follows.

> *All business income losses are settled based on the coverage limit purchased. An accurate business income coverage limit calculation depends on an accurate estimation of the 12-month business income exposure and the legitimate estimation of the worst-case period of restoration. Estimating the worst-case period of restoration necessitates understanding the time required to accomplish each of the 10 steps within the four period of restoration objectives. The key to business income is the correct estimation of time.*

Importance of these Terms and Concepts

Business income, period of restoration, operational capability, and the time doctrine are referenced throughout the remainder of this book. All other concepts surrounding business income coverage are built on these four terms and concepts. Knowing and understanding these concepts simplifies and demystifies business income coverage.

Chapter 3

Business Income's Key Policy Provisions

Nine pages! The business income form is a mere nine pages, but these few pages encompass what has historically been confusing, scary, and undersold.

Chapter 2 introduced four key BI concepts. This chapter details the four key business income policy coverage provisions that must be known and understood before digging into the policy specifics. The four provisions follow.

- The three income sources the form can protect
- The five required coverage triggers
- The requirement that there be a covered cause of loss
- A description of how a business income loss is determined

Three Business Income Source Options

Three sources of income are "coverable" by the business income policy; and "rental value" seems to be a key component of these options.

- Business Income (BI) <u>including</u> Rental Value (RV)
- Business Income <u>other than</u> Rental Value
- Rental Value (only)

Business Income including Rental Value is often the choice of insureds that occupy part of the building and lease out part. *Business Income other than Rental Value* is selected if the insured receives no rental income from use of the insured building. Pure *Rental Value* coverage generally applies to a lessor's risk only-type policy.

As the name suggests, "rental value" is income the insured receives from contracted tenants who lease or rent space in the insured structure. The insured has the option to insure the loss of rents as part of the business income, on a stand-alone basis or not at all. Insureds choosing to not protect the loss of rental income generally transfer the loss of rent exposure to the tenant via the lease agreement.

Rental value is captured on Line G of the business income report/worksheet (CP 15 15). Line G reads "Other earnings from your business operations (not investment income or rents from other properties)." Only rents received from the insured location are contemplated.

Five Business Income Coverage Triggers

"A.1." of both business income coverage forms (CP 00 30 and CP 00 32) specifies the five coverage triggers. Business income loss is payable only if all the following requirements are met.

- There must be a suspension of operations (total or partial).

- The policy only pays for income lost during the period of restoration (Period of Restoration is detailed in Chapter 5).
- The suspension must be caused by direct physical loss of or damage to property at an insured premises.
- The damage or destruction must be caused by a covered cause of loss (based on the cause of loss form attached).
- If personal property in the open (or in a vehicle) causes a suspension of operations, such property must be located within 100 feet of the insured premises for BI coverage to apply. (Often extended to 1000 feet in proprietary forms.)

Covered Cause of Loss

Business income coverage applies (and the loss is paid) only if the damage to or destruction of insured property emanates from a covered cause of loss. The business income policy references and employs the same cause of loss form used by the commercial property policy (either the special, broad or basic form).

There are additional exclusions specific to Business Income/Extra Expense (BI/EE) coverage (and not applicable to the other commercial property coverages) are found in all three causes of loss forms.

- No business income coverage is available to pay for damage to or destruction of finished stock.

- The period of restoration does not include time to replace or repair finished stock (see Chapter 5).
- Business income or extra expense coverage is not available if the business suspension is caused by or the result of damage to or destruction of any part of a radio or television antenna (can be covered by attachment of the CP 15 50 endorsement – see Chapter 14).
- The period of restoration does not include any increase in building time due to the actions of strikers or any other like persons.
- The period of restoration is not lengthened due simply to the suspense, lapse or cancellation of any license, lease or contract. Any increase in the business income loss resulting from such suspension, lapse or cancellation directly caused by the suspension of operations IS covered, but only during the original period of restoration and any extended business income or extended period of indemnity.
- No extra expense protection is provided due to the suspension, lapse or cancellation of any license, lease or contract.

Loss Determination

How is the amount of compensable business income loss determined following a business closing loss? (Chapter 9 details the difference between insurable and compensable business income.) The policy form itself attempts to provide an applicable framework to assist in developing the correct answer, but the policy form's directions may create confusion rather than clarity.

According to the policy, the amount of business income payment is determined by the following steps.

1. Analyzing the insured's "net income" before the business-closing loss occurred. What was happening with the income? Was it trending up? Was it trending down?

2. Anticipating or estimating the insured's likely "net income" during the period of restoration had no loss occurred. Such estimation is not only a function of the trends prior to the loss, but also the history of the business during the period of restoration. Was the business forced to close during its normal busy season (peak season)? If so, the peak season must be considered in estimating the loss of net income.

3. Totaling all operating expenses "necessary to resume operations." The policy states that these operating expenses include payroll expenses. This provision causes many misunderstandings and is often misapplied at the time of a claims settlement. The wording does not limit and is not intended to limit coverage for operating expenses or payroll expense to only those expenses or employees "necessary" to resume operations. This provision is intended to highlight the fact that business income coverage is intended to include any additional operating expenses not usual and customary to the operation, including

payroll, necessary to resume operational capability. An example is overtime pay for employees necessary to help the entity resume operations (as this may not be a usual and customary operating expense). This differs appreciably from extra expense coverage (see Chapter 11).

4. Reviewing all other relevant financial information necessary to determine the amount of loss such as: financial records, bills, invoices, deeds, liens, contracts, etc.

Combine this policy provision with the definition of "business income" found in the policy to get a better picture of the amount paid following a business income loss. The definition of "business income" and the Loss Determination policy wording directly or by inference share several terms and concepts in common.

- "Net income": Net profit (or loss) before tax. The definition of business income and the loss determination policy provision both use the term net income.
- "Continuing normal operating expenses": Normal, usual, or customary operating expenses that continue in whole or in part during the period of restoration. This phrase is found within the definition of business income only, but it is inferred in the loss determination language when the form states that all financial records, bills, invoices, liens, contracts, etc. are to be

considered. Those financial documents contain the information necessary to prove continuing normal operating expenses, including continuing payroll expenses not removed by attachment of the CP 15 10 (discussed in Chapter 4).

- "Operating expenses, including payroll expenses, necessary to resume operations": These are not the normal, usual, and customary expenses that continue during the period of restoration; these are unusual operating expenses (not extra expenses, which are non-operational expenses) necessary to resume operational capability. This phrase is found only in the loss determination section of the policy, it is not found in the definition of business income (which is what the policy is supposed to pay). Thus, it is evident that this provision refers to operating or payroll expenses not usual and customary but extra-ordinary operating or payroll expenses necessary to resume operational capability. This is not intended to limit coverage for employee payroll to only those "necessary" to resume operations (unless the CP 15 10 is attached). Why is this provision not equivalent to extra expense coverage? Because extra expense generally involves costs associated with temporary measures at the same or another location to allow some level of operational continuity – non-operational expenses. The expenses referred to in the loss determination section relate to permanent measures at the permanent location necessary to return to operational capability. See Chapter 11 for more detail on extra expense coverage.

Chapter 4

Understanding the Business Income Worksheet

Few agents seek to introduce (much less discuss) the business income report/worksheet with clients. The prospect of handing the client a six-page document with dozens of blank lines and asking them to provide what the client views as private and confidential financial information discourages many agents from attempting to recommend this most important coverage.

Fear of having to actually explain the business income report/worksheet (CP 15 15) leaves all but the most hardcore agents cowering in the corner. Granted, this assertion may be hyperbole, but not by much. The CP 15 15 (the *Business Income Report/Worksheet*) can be a scary document, especially when its purpose and mechanics are not fully understood.

The Reason for the Business Income Worksheet

Commercial property underwriters generally require the insured to provide a current property schedule detailing the locations, square footage, construction, occupancy, building values and content values being insured, along with any other information the underwriter deems important. This is exactly what the business income worksheet is: the time element (business income) equivalent of the commercial property schedule detailing the qualified business income exposure the underwriter is being asked to insure.

The worksheet/report is nothing more than the starting point in the business income underwriting process. It is designed to calculate the estimated 12-month "business income" exposure and ultimately lead the insured to the correct amount of coverage developed by applying the maximum coinsurance percentage (Chapter 6), which is based on the estimated period of restoration (Chapter 5), to the 12-month business income exposure developed by the worksheet.

Completing the Worksheet

Insureds need not complete every line of the business income report/worksheet. Generally, only two of the four columns, based on the classification of the insured, require completion. Manufacturing operations complete the first and third columns; non-manufacturing insureds use the second and fourth columns. Dual purpose operations, however, do complete all four columns (as detailed later in this chapter).

The first applicable column, first or second based on entity type, provides details about the 12-month financial period ending the last day of the current policy period. The second column completed by the insured (the third or fourth) is an estimate of the upcoming 12-month coverage (policy) period.

Of the two, the column providing the estimate for the upcoming 12 months (the third or fourth column based on entity type) is the more important. Business income coverage protects the insured against income losses experienced during the current policy year, not based on what occurred in the prior year.

Likewise, coinsurance penalties are assessed based on the actual financial data of the current policy year, not on the previous 12 months, so an accurate estimate of the coming 12 months is of utmost importance. Whether the estimated figures are developed using trending, models, or gut feeling really doesn't matter; the only necessity is that the estimate closely mirror reality at the time of loss.

Both manufacturing and non-manufacturing insureds can find most of the information necessary to complete the CP 15 15 on the most current fiscal year-end income statement. However, the business income report/worksheet does contain a few non-GAAP (Generally Accepted Accounting Principles) calculations detailed in this chapter.

The estimate for the upcoming 12 months is basically a combination of the budgeting process and best-guess market projections.

Important Business Income Worksheet Definitions

Business income report/worksheet terms are defined then described in the following paragraphs. Each factor's calculation methodology is presented to provide a better understanding of how the CP 15 15 develops the total insurable business income (see Chapter 9 for a detailed discussion of the difference between "compensable" and "insurable" business income).

The insured's classification as a manufacturing or non-manufacturing entity alters the meaning of certain terms (as presented in the worksheet) or requires the use of different factors in the calculation of a particular figure. Where the definitions or calculations differ, the variations are explained. Some terms apply strictly to one or the other operational type; those differences are likewise specified and detailed.

Page 1: Although no calculations are done on the first page of the CP 15 15, a very important piece of information is found here: The accrual basis of accounting is required by the CP 15 15 in the calculation of the 12-month business income exposure. Each definition presented in this chapter satisfies this requirement.

Calculating Total Revenues

Lines A through H on page 2 of the business income report/ worksheet develop the total insured's total revenues (as defined by the CP 15 15). Again, there are two columns, one for the current information and the second for the estimated exposure. Each line is detailed in this section.

While Line A of the CP 15 15 is common to both risk types — manufacturing and non-manufacturing risks — lines "B," "C," and "D" apply to only manufacturing risks. But both risk types are required to complete the last four lines/sections of the worksheet's revenue calculation section on page 2. Lines/sections E through H use essentially the same data for both risk types of operations with one noted exception in the development of "net sales" (Line F).

Gross Sales: Line A applies to both manufacturing and non-manufacturing operations and can be found on the insured's income statement. It is the value of all invoices collected by the insured or billed by the insured during the referenced period before customer discounts, allowances, or returns.

Finished Stock Inventory at the Beginning of the Year (at <u>sales</u> value): Line B applies to only manufacturing operations. The sales value of finished stock at the beginning of the year is subtracted from gross sales. GAAP-compliant income statements generally do not specify the internal value (cost) of finished stock on hand from which the sales value of finished stock can be deciphered; a Cost of Goods Sold (COGS) Statement or separate internal calculation is likely required.

Developing the sales value of finished stock requires the beginning inventory to be divided into three component parts: 1) the cost of raw materials; 2) stock in process; and 3) finished stock value (internal cost). This breakdown is not an additional step, as the figures are required to arrive at the CP 15 15's definition of COGS (the form's unique calculation of COGS is detailed later in this chapter).

Once inventory is divided into these component parts, at least two methods can be applied to the internal value of finished stock to develop the sales value of finished stock on hand, the "mark-up" margin method and the "percentage-of-net-sales" calculation.

1. "Mark up" (margin) method. The cost (internal value) of finished stock on hand and the desired profit margin

are the primary factors in this calculation. The insured multiplies the cost of finished stock on hand by one plus the desired or normal "mark-up" (desired profit margin) percentage. For example, if the finished stock cost is $100,000 and the desired profit margin is 33.3%; the "sales value" of the finished stock is $133,300 ($100,000 x (1+33.3%)).

2. The "percentage-of-net-sales" (percentage) calculation. This method may prove to be less accurate than the mark-up method; but the result should be fairly close as it tends to follow the same "margin" logic as the "mark-up" method, just from the opposite direction. The traditional COGS is divided by the net sales (COGS/NS) (net sales is "gross sales" less returns and allowances) producing the cost of goods sold ratio (COGSR). The cost of the finished stock is divided by the COGSR, yielding the estimated sales value of finished stock on hand at the beginning of the calculation period. For example, if the COGS is $1,000,000 and the net sales is $1,500,000; the COGS ratio is 0.67. If the cost of finished stock on hand is $100,000; the sales value of that stock is approximately $149,254 ($100,000/0.67).

Calculating the sales value of finished stock on hand may be best accomplished by using both methods. Because GAAP standards and the CP 15 15's calculation method do not match, a best guess estimate using the average of the two calculations may deliver the best and most accurate result.

Finished Stock Inventory at the End of the Year (at sales value): Line C also applies solely to manufacturing risks. The sales value of finished stock on hand at the end of the fiscal period is added to the gross sales. Developing this value is complicated by the same problems inherent in the calculation of the sales value of finished stock at the beginning of the year. Both the mark up method and the percentage-of-net-sales method can be applied to the internal value (cost) of the finished stock on hand at the end of the fiscal period to estimate the year-end sales value of finished stock on hand.

Gross Sales Value of Production: Line D applies to only manufacturing risks. This is the result of Gross Sales (Line A) minus Finished Stock Inventory at the Beginning of the Year (Line B) plus the Finished Stock Inventory at the End of the Year (Line C).

As the name suggests, Line D captures the maximum possible revenues represented by the recorded period's 12 months of production, whether the finished product was sold or sits in stock. In essence, this value represents the revenue the insured would have earned if every item produced during that 12-month period was sold, leaving nothing in stock (no excess production).

Insurable business income for manufacturing risks is based on actual accrued sales plus the potential accrued sales (represented by production output during the year). Essentially, the worksheet cannot and does not ignore the potential that the insured may (or might) sell 100% of its finished stock.

Cost of Sales, Unrealized Income, and Collection Expenses

Section "E" applies to both manufacturing and non-manufacturing insureds. Three categories of expenses and costs are captured in this section: 1) sales expenses; 2) unrealized income; and 3) collection expenses.

Cost of Sales: As the title suggests, these are sales-related expenses that must be deducted from gross sales value of production for manufacturing risks or gross sales for non-manufacturing risks to ultimately develop the net sales value of production (for manufacturers) or net sales (for non-manufacturing operation). Pre-paid outgoing freight, returns and allowances, and discounts are "costs" associated with the post-production sales process, and thus reduce the amount of revenues and ultimate realized income available to pay operating costs. These costs, presumably, do not continue after a loss, with the possible exception of costs associated with a return (i.e. a buyer returns a purchase within a specified time expecting a refund), because there is no (or limited) production and/or sales.

Bad Debt: Bad debt is money due that cannot be collected. Because the business income worksheet is completed on an accrual basis (rather than a cash basis), bad debt is unrealized income included in the gross sales figure and must be deducted to accurately generate the true revenues available to operate the business.

Collection Expenses: Like bad debt, collection expenses reduce the amount of cash available to cover business-related expenses and generate a profit. Collection expenses reported in the business income worksheet represent the cost of outside collection agencies or other third parties hired to recover payment from buyers. This deduction does not exclude from revenues the costs of employees involved in debt collection.

Bad debt and collection expenses may actually increase following a business-closing loss. Those that usually pay may simply decide to wait (to see if the business reopens) or not pay at all; and those that are habitually slow payers decide to wait longer than usual or, again, not pay at all. Both situations may push the insured to hire a collection agency and/or write off more debt than normal.

Are these increases in bad debt and collection expenses to be excluded from compensable business income because the costs are being deducted during the calculation process? If the letter and apparent intent of the policy wording is followed, any increase in bad debt and/or collection expense should be covered within the definition of business income.

The business income policy states that loss is determined based in part on the "*likely Net Income ... if no physical loss or damage had occurre*d." If the insured historically and consistently experiences bad debt and collection expenses equal to 3% of total revenue, yet that number jumps to 6% following a business-closing loss, the additional 3% is logically attributable to the shut-down. The insured should be able to successfully argue that any spike in bad debt and/or collection expenses logically attributable to a business-closing loss negatively affecting the "likely net income," and thus should be part of the compensable business income.

Cost of sales, unrealized income, and collection expenses are subtracted from the ultimate business income calculation because they are purportedly non-continuing operational expenses, directly related to the sales process (a.k.a. non-continuing sales-related operational costs). Without sales there should be no sales expenses.

Net Sales (non-manufacturing)/Net Sales Value of Production (manufacturing): Line F is gross sales (Line A) minus sales expenses, bad debt, and collection expenses (section E) for non-manufacturing operations; and gross sales value of production (line D) minus sales expenses, bad debt, and collection expenses (section E) for manufacturing operations.

Other Earnings: Section G allows the insured to account for earnings not related to sales. Such earnings may include commissions or rents, cash discounts received, or any other non-sales earnings with a few exceptions (exceptions include investment income and rental income from other properties).

Business income is largely location-specific coverage; there are options for blanket protection, but only if specific requirements are met. Because of this, the only "other" income the insurance carrier expects to be listed on the CP 15 15 is income directly related to the presence of the insured building or buildings (when blanket coverage is allowed). Presumably, investment income continues to flow in even if the building is not there. Likewise, the destruction of the building(s) at the insured location does not (or should not) lower rental income from owned property at another location (provided the rental property is located someplace else).

An important term in this section is "your." The worksheet requests that the named insured(s) add other earnings "from 'your' business operations." To be included in this calculation, the eligible other income must be assignable to the policy's defined "you."

Total Revenues: All this adding and subtracting results in the insured's total revenue as defined by the business income form. This value is entered on Line "H" at the bottom of page 2 of the worksheet and is carried over to the top of page 3.

Subtracting Expenses:
Developing the Actual Business Income Exposure

With total revenues calculated, the business income report/worksheet moves to the form's expense section on page 3. Five non-continuing, production-related expense categories are subtracted from total revenues (Line H) to produce the insured's 12-month business income exposure. These are: 1) cost of goods sold (COGS); 2) outside services resold; 3) utility services that do not continue under contract; 4) payroll of specified workers; and 5) special deductions for mining operations.

Two of the five expense categories apply only if specific endorsements are attached, and the last applies only when the insured is a mining operation.

Cost of Goods Sold (COGS) - A Required Deduction

Cost of Goods Sold is developed for both manufacturing and non-manufacturing risks with only minor calculation differences between the two operational types. Most of the information necessary to develop COGS can be found on the insured's income statement. However, standard income statements follow generally accepted accounting principles (GAAP) requirements while the business income report/worksheet strays from the GAAP when calculating a manufacturer's COGS.

Two distinct differences exist between the GAAP method for calculating a manufacturer's COGS and the business income worksheet's method for calculating COGS.

- GAAP-calculated COGS includes the competed value of finished stock on hand when developing both beginning and ending inventory values. The value of finished stock on hand is excluded from the CP 15 15's COGS calculation.
- GAAP-calculated COGS includes the cost of labor directly related to production. Production-related labor costs are specifically excluded in CP 15 15's COGS calculation.

Both costs included in a GAAP income statement but excluded from the CP 15 15 are applied and accounted for in other parts of the business income worksheet as follows.

- Beginning and ending finished stock inventory values are used to develop the Gross Sales Value of Production in the income section of the business income worksheet (Lines B and C).
- Production-related labor costs are classified as "payroll" and subject to a specific endorsement (the CP 15 10). The insured may include all or only part of payroll as an ongoing expense. The CP 15 10 is detailed in an upcoming section.

These income statement and business income worksheet differences prevent the insured from simply copying COGS information directly from the income statement onto the business income worksheet's COGS calculation found on page 5 of the form.

Like the business income report/worksheet, the insured completes the COGS information for the most recently ended 12-month period and estimates the information for the upcoming 12 months (the policy period). The calculation is as follows.

1. Inventory at the beginning of the year
2. Plus (+): The cost of raw stock purchased during the year
3. Plus (+): The cost of factory supplies consumed
4. Plus (+): The cost of merchandise sold

5. Plus (+): The cost of other supplies consumed

6. Equals (=): The cost of goods available for sale

7. Minus (-): Inventory on hand at the end of the year

8. Equals (=): Cost of goods sold

Step 1. Remember, manufacturing operations do not include the cost/value of finished stock on hand in this figure. Only raw stock and stock-in-process are included.

Step 2. This is not provided by non-manufacturing operations.

Step 3. This is not provided by non-manufacturing operations.

Step 4. This is the cost of stock/inventory purchased and held for sale by non-manufacturing operations. For manufacturers, this is the cost of merchandise manufactured by another party but sold by the insured.

Step 5. This is the cost of supplies consumed but not made part of the manufactured product. Examples include safety equipment (i.e. gloves, ear plugs, etc.), oil for machinery, and other such supplies.

Step 6. Self-explanatory.

Step 7. Remember, the cost/value of finished stock on hand is excluded from this amount for manufacturing operations. This amount represents the cost of raw materials plus stock in process on hand at the end of the year.

Step 8. The total carried over to the COGS line in Section "I."

Steps two and three apply only to manufacturing risks. Step four is the cost of inventory for non-manufacturing operations; but for manufacturing risks it is the cost of goods manufactured by others and sold by the manufacturer (i.e. a product accessory stocked and sold but not manufactured by the insured).

Not all entities require a COGS calculation. Those that neither produce nor sell a tangible product (for example, insurance agencies, law firms, consultants, and accountants), or those that purchase only rental income protection may not need a COGS calculation.

Outside Services Resold - A Required Deduction

The cost of outside services resold by the insured is the second non-continuing, production-related expense required to be deducted from total revenue. Examples of such expenses may include services offered by outside engineers in performing plan review (stamped plans), the cost of subcontractors hired by the insured to perform specific tasks, or the cost of independent consultants the insured pays directly but charges back to the client as part of its total services.

Assume the insured is a structural steel fabricator and one of the services offered is structural engineer plan review, but only when the insured is providing the steel. Because there is no engineer on staff, all review is done by a third-party engineer (an independent contractor). The cost of the engineer is paid by the fabricator and passed along to the customer, with a small markup. If the manufacturer ceases operation because of a major loss, the cost of those contracted engineering services is deducted from revenue because there is theoretically no need for the service when there is no manufacturing.

This deduction has two caveats: 1) The services have to be those that are resold to the insured's customers. This is not a deduction for services purchased by the insured for the insured's own use (such as consulting services); and 2) The service has to end when production ceases (i.e. if there is a contract that requires continued payment even when no work is being given, the insured does not deduct those costs).

Utility Services - An Optional Deduction

Power, heat, and refrigeration expenses that do not continue following a loss-induced business shut-down per a contract between the utility and the insured can be deducted from total revenues, but only if the CP 15 11 is attached. The CP 15 11 applies only to utility services related to production operations, so this is essentially a manufacturing-specific endorsement.

Manufacturing operations that consume large amounts of one or all of these listed services may enter into a contract with the utility provider for reduced rates and/or a more predictable payment schedule, rather than struggle with fluctuating costs that are difficult to anticipate. If the agreement allows the insured to cease payments in the event of a business shut-down, the CP 15 11 should be attached, and the deduction taken.

However, if the insured must make payments regardless of the business' operational status, the endorsement should not be attached; and if it is, it won't apply because the payments continue. Essentially, contracted utility payments that continue after a loss become part of continuing normal operating expenses.

Payroll - An Optional Deduction

Does the insured want or need to keep all or any employees on staff during a loss-induced business shut-down? Business entities requiring specially trained employees that cannot be easily replaced may want to keep everyone on staff and paid until the business returns to operational capability. But some operations may not require highly skilled workers, or they may operate in an area with ample talent leading the employer to decide to let some, several, or all employees go during the shut-down, choosing to rehire the employees once the business is again operational.

Insureds who believe some or all employees are unnecessary during the period of operational shut down (the period of restoration) may choose to attach the CP 15 10 - Payroll Limitation or Exclusion. This endorsement, revised by ISO in 2013, is somewhat customizable. When attached, the insured makes two key decisions: 1) which employees are to be paid by the business income coverage; and 2) how long, if at all, is protection extended to cover the payroll of employees who may be considered non-essential and thus excluded from coverage.

Regarding choice one, which employees to cover; the endorsement offers several options.

- All employees and job classifications including officers, executives, management personnel, and contract employees.
- All employees and job classifications other than officers, executives, management personnel, and contract employees.
- All employees and job classifications (including officers, executives, management personnel and contract employees), except: (the exceptions are listed).
- Only the following job classifications and/or employees: (list those to be excluded).

Once the insured decides who to cover and who to exclude, the insured has the option of choosing a time limit of protection for those employees to be excluded from full protection. Yes, the insured can cover the payroll of excluded employees for some specified period of time (in the event the loss has a short period of restoration), but end payment at a predetermined point. The available options are 90 and 180 days. This choice is not required; the employer/insured can choose to exclude the payroll of the specified employees in full (for the entire period of restoration).

"**Payroll**" in this context is: Payroll + Employee Benefits (directly related to payroll) + FICA payments + Union Dues + Workers' Compensation premiums.

Historically, prior to the 2013 revision, this exclusionary endorsement applied to only "ordinary employees." An ordinary employee was defined as an employee not classified as an officer, executive, department manager, employee under contract, or any specifically listed employee or job description. With the 2013 revision of this endorsement, this is no longer the case.

Special Deductions for Mining Operations - A Required Deduction

Certain expenses are deducted when the insured is a mining operation. These are royalties (unless specifically included), actual depletion, welfare and retirement fund charges based on tonnage, and hired trucks. The sum of those expenses is moved to the last line of Section I deductions.

Obviously, if the insured is not a mining property, this section on page 6 of the CP 15 15 does not apply.

How All Deductible Costs and Expenses Apply

Non-continuing, sales-related operational costs (in Section "E") plus the non-continuing, production-related expenses (Section "I") are the only costs/expenses specifically subtracted from gross sales (or gross sales value of production) and total revenues (respectively) in the development of the insured's 12-month business income exposure. This is important when viewed in context with the definition of

business income (*net income (net profit or loss before tax)*
plus continuing normal operating expenses).

Until a loss occurs, the insured is not charged with
knowing or deciding which operational expenses will continue,
will not continue, or will be reduced. Attempting to pinpoint
continuing and non-continuing expenses prior to a loss serves
only to complicate and confuse the process; it's pointless and,
more importantly, unnecessary. Not contemplating continuing
and non-continuing operational expenses at this point does
create a difference between insurable (ratable) business
income and compensable business income. The difference can
confuse or anger the insured if not properly explained. The
concept of and difference between insurable and compensable
business income are discussed and detailed in Chapter 9.

The 12-Month BI Exposure

Line J is simply the total net revenue developed in Line "H"
minus production-related expenses – the 12-month business
income exposure. With this amount and an honest estimation
of the time necessary to resume operational capability
following a worst-case loss, two calculations can be made: 1)
the correct coinsurance percentage can be calculated (as
detailed in Chapter 6); and 2) the correct amount of business
income coverage can be calculated.

Why Two "Js"

Before moving forward, the purpose and reason for the two
"J" lines must be clarified. Although explained in the CP 15 15,
the reason deserves attention.

If the insured is solely a manufacturing operation or exclusively a non-manufacturing operation, "J.2." can be ignored. Line "J.2." is necessary only when the insured is a dual-purpose operation; that is, it receives income from both manufacturing and non-manufacturing operations that are not directly relatable to the manufacturing process (i.e. a retail outlet not selling the manufactured goods).

A dual-purpose operation must complete all four columns of the worksheet, the manufacturing and non-manufacturing financial data. "Single-purpose" operations, which are most frequently the case, need only complete the two columns detailed at the beginning of Chapter 4 and provide the "J.1." total.

Note that the J.1. (or J.2. if a dual-purpose operation) amount is the total business income exposure for a 12-month period. This fact becomes important as the coinsurance percentage and the limit of coverage are developed.

The two remaining lines on page 4 of the business income report/worksheet — the *Extra Expense amount (K.1")*; and *the Extended Business Income/Extended Period of Indemnity (K.2.)* — are not discussed in this chapter. A detailed discussion of those concepts and coverages is left for chapters 8 (K.2.) and 11 (K.1.).

Next Steps

Developing the 12-month business income exposure using the CP 15 15 is the first in a three-step process towards the goal of protecting the entity's income stream following a business-closing loss. The next step is the most important and the most difficult, estimating the worst-case period of restoration.

Business income coinsurance is a function of a properly estimated period of restoration. The ultimately chosen business income limit is primarily a function of the period of restoration and secondarily a function of the coinsurance percentage. A correct period of restoration calculation is imperative.

Chapters 4, 5, 6, and 7 should be taken as a package, a mini-book within a book. There are four calculations to properly protect the insured's income following a loss.

- Correctly calculate the 12-month business income exposure (Chapter 4).
- Properly estimate the worst-case period of restoration (Chapter 5).
- Calculate the proper coinsurance percentage (Chapter 6).
- Calculate the correct amount of business income coverage (Chapter 7).

Chapter 5
Business Income's 'Period of Restoration'

Period of Restoration carries essentially the same definition in all three ISO time element forms, with a slight variation in the CP 00 50 (since it provides only extra expense coverage).

F.3. "Period of restoration" means the period of time that:
a) Begins:
(1) 72 hours after the time of direct physical loss or damage for Business Income Coverage; or
(2) Immediately after the time of direct physical loss or damage for Extra Expense Coverage; caused by or resulting from any Covered Cause of Loss at the described premises; and
b) Ends on the earlier of:
(1) The date when the property at the described premises should be repaired, rebuilt or replaced with reasonable speed and similar quality; or
(2) The date when business is resumed at a new permanent location.
Period of restoration does not include any increased period required due to the enforcement of any ordinance or law that:

(1) Regulates the construction, use or repair, or requires the tearing down, of any property; or

(2) Requires any insured or others to test for, monitor, clean-up, remove, contain, treat, detoxify or neutralize, in any way respond to, or assess the effects of "pollutants".

The expiration date of this policy will not cut short the period of restoration.

Four key objectives must be accomplished as quickly as reasonably possible during the period of restoration.

1. Rebuild the building or find and move to an alternate permanent location.
2. Find, purchase, install, and have operational new or used replacement machinery and equipment.
3. Replace and/or replenish stock (does not include "finished stock" for manufacturing operations).
4. Return to the same level of "operational capability" existing just prior to the loss.

The goal of the first three objectives is to realize the final objective as quickly as possible, returning the business to its pre-loss operational capability. Speed is of the essence in completing all four objectives. Remember, the policy specifically states that coverage ends when the property "should be repaired..." and not when it "is repaired." Dragging out the return to operational capability without due cause or need risks the loss of additional income for which no protection is provided.

Establishing the Period of Restoration

Estimating the period of restoration (POR), the time required to accomplish all four POR objectives, is the first step toward developing the maximum coinsurance percentage and the necessary coverage limits (as detailed in Chapter 6). A proper and honest assessment of the period of restoration leads to the establishment of the correct coinsurance choice and ultimately the business income coverage limits (provided the business income report/worksheet is completed accurately). Any underestimation of the POR may be detrimental to the insured's income and ongoing operations.

The period of restoration, as defined in the coverage form, is a moving target that fluctuates based on the amount of damage, the time of year, whether the loss is individual or communal, and many other factors. Insureds should assume a worst-case scenario loss (a total or constructive total loss to the insured premises at the worst possible time) when planning and purchasing business income coverage.

Ten Factors that Directly Affect the Period of Restoration

Attempting to properly estimate the period of restoration requires a clear understanding of all factors that directly control the time required to complete the four stated POR objectives. There are 10 time-factors that affect the time required.

1. The direct property loss must be adjusted.
2. Building plans have to be drawn and approved.
3. A contractor must be found and hired.

4. The insured must apply, wait for, and be granted building permits.

5. Site preparation must be scheduled and completed, including clearing the site of damaged or destroyed property (and maybe even undamaged property).

6. The time required to rebuild (the length may be adversely affected by No. 10).

7. The time required to restock.

8. Rehiring and hiring new employees.

9. Replacement machinery and equipment must be found, purchased, installed, and made operational.

10. The federal, state or local government may become involved following a loss.

This is likely not an all-inclusive time-factor list, nor is it in order of importance or time consumption. The list is also non-linear, meaning that several steps can and may be completed simultaneously.

The Importance of the List

Correct calculation of BI's coinsurance percentage (detailed in Chapter 6) requires a thorough understanding of the four period of restoration objectives and the 10 incremental steps necessary to accomplish the objectives. Accurately estimating the time required to return the business to its full operational capability is key to establishing the maximum coinsurance percentage, the amount subject to loss, and finally the minimum amount of business income coverage to purchase. As stated, developing the maximum coinsurance percentage is easy; estimating the basis for that choice, the period of restoration, is difficult.

The Reality of the Period of Restoration

Successfully completing all four period-of-restoration (POR) objectives and returning to operational capability as quickly as possible requires the insured navigate many obstacles and potential delays. Building owners likely do not understand or are unaware of everything that must be accomplished before the structure is or even can be rebuilt. Because of this lack of understanding, these owners often underestimate reality.

To allow for a better understanding of the reality of the period of restoration Each of the 10 time-factors listed previously are discussed in detail over the next several paragraphs.

Direct Loss Property Adjustment

Before any other step in the period of restoration process can begin, the direct property loss must be adjusted or be in the process of adjustment. This time drain cannot be overlooked when calculating the period of restoration. Remember, this is just the time necessary to adjust the loss on the building, the business income loss adjustment timing is not even considered at this point.

How long will the direct loss adjustment take? Forty-five days is the likely minimum, but this process will likely devour closer to 60 or even 90 days following the loss (sometimes longer). Justifying this estimate requires a review of the property loss adjustment process.

Immediately following the loss and the insurance carrier's notification of the damage, the insured must prove the amount of loss by submitting a proof of loss form to the insurance carrier. The proof of loss requires the insured to schedule and provide values for each item or item group of damaged property (building and contents). Insureds are allowed 60 days from the day the insurance carrier provides the form to complete and return the proof of loss to the carrier. The time spent completing the proof of loss is up to the insured.

Once the property insurer receives the proof of loss, policy provisions allow the carrier up to 30 days to review the information and decide whether all the necessary data and proof is present, allowing it to go ahead and settle the loss. If the carrier has the necessary documentation and is convinced that the insured's claim is accurate, payment is made within that same 30-day review process.

However, should the insurance carrier disagree with the insured's valuation or doubt the insured's account of events, it may deny the claim as submitted and/or offer some amount less than what is claimed. This begins the appraisal process.

Estimating the timing required to go through the full appraisal process is a guess. Interestingly, ISO's commercial property policy states that even if there is an appraisal decision, the insurance carrier still has the right to deny the claim.

If the appraisal results are acceptable to the insured, the insurance carrier is to pay the decided upon amount within 30 days of the finding. But should the appraisal process fail to satisfy the insured, the courts may be called upon to settle the matter. How long the process might take is an unknown.

This broad overview lacks many details making up the direct property loss adjustment process but knowing the realities of the process gives the insured a better starting point from which to estimate the legitimate period of restoration.

Keep in mind, other steps toward the entity's return to operational capability can be accomplished during the adjustment process (i.e. finding replacement equipment, developing building plans, interviewing and selecting a general contractor, and maybe preliminary site preparation). This is not a dead time where nothing else can occur.

For sake of the period of restoration process, allow 60 to 75 .days minimum for the property loss adjustment. Alter the length based on the size and distinctive features of the property, complexity of the operations, and uniqueness of the machinery and equipment.

Pre-Construction Period of Restoration Time Factors

During the direct property loss adjustment process, the insured can initiate some of the non-building/pre-construction requirements that are necessary preliminaries to rebuilding.

- Development and approval of the new building plans.
- Advertising for, interviewing, and selecting a general contractor.

- Applying for and waiting on building permits.
- Scheduling and completing site clearance work.

Development and Approval of Building Plans:

Before the building can be rebuilt, building plans must be drawn, approved by the insured, and, in many cases, approved by a governmental authority. The three parts of this process may require 60, 90, 120, or more days based on complexity and the bureaucracy to which the insured is subject. The good news is a large portion of this can be accomplished during the adjustment process.

Advertising for, Interviewing, and Choosing a General Contractor:

This step, too, can begin during the adjustment process. The time required to accomplish this step is a function of current economic conditions, the quality of the general contractor pool, and the necessity of a specially trained general contractor. Once begun, the process could take as long as 45 days, but not in every case.

Applying for and Waiting on Building Permits:

This process may not be as burdensome as it once was. Some jurisdictional building departments report turnaround times of 15 business days. The top-end estimate for this part is 30 days. This includes the time for the insured to acquire the form(s), complete the information and receive the building permit. However, this step cannot be accomplished in the absence of the building plans, so this is linearly dependent on the receipt of the final building plans.

Scheduling and Completing the Site Clearance Work: Work cannot begin on the new building until the site has been cleared and prepared for construction. Site clearing cannot be done until specific milestones are accomplished: 1) a demolition contractor has to be found; 2) the demolition has to be scheduled (may be 15 to 30 days before the chosen contractor can do the work); 3) the insurance carrier has to approve the clearance of the site; and 4) the appropriate governmental authorities have to approve the site clearance.

Site clearance and preparation can be slowed by the adjustment process and bureaucratic issues. If the insured and the insurance carrier have not settled the loss, the carrier may hold up this part of the pre-construction process to preserve evidence for the appraisal process. Likewise, one of many governmental entities may not allow the building owner to begin clearing the site until specific reviews and/or studies have been completed (i.e. the U.S. Environmental Protection Agency). Governmental involvement is more completely detailed later in this chapter.

Getting past all four site-clearance milestones may add an additional 30 to 45 days to the process, depending on various external unknowns.

Completing all the pre-construction requirements highlighted above may add between 45 and 60 days to the already-spent adjustment process time. The insured may have already invested somewhere between three and five months in the rebuilding process before the footings of the replacement building have even been placed.

Again, understand that the presented time periods are estimates and assume a worst-case-scenario loss. Some parts of the process to this point may be shortened with others drawn out. Each loss is influenced by individualized circumstances, but the insured must be cognizant of the real issues and time factors involved in pre-construction.

Time Required to Rebuild the Structure

Too many factors directly affect the time required to rebuild a structure to hazard a guess at the time required to rebuild any structure. The size of the building, special features, weather conditions, economic conditions, availability of skilled labor, unforeseen accidents, availability of materials, and many other issues play a part in the time necessary to rebuild a structure.

For sake of the discussion, assume four months on the short (very short) side and eight months on the long side. Again, these are just mid-point guesses. Adjust the estimate to fit the insured and its building.

When quizzed about the time necessary to rebuild the structure, many insureds tend to think only about and plan only for the actual building phase, ignoring the adjustment and pre-construction time requirements. If the insured states that six months is required to rebuild, he is probably right, but only from the point at which all the adjustment and preliminary work has been completed. Add the adjustment time, pre-building requirements, and the time necessary to actually rebuild the structure to develop a true estimate of the time that will pass between the loss and when the building can be occupied and operational. An overestimate is preferable to an underestimate.

Restocking - Two Definitions

Neither manufacturing nor non-manufacturing operations can return to full operational capability until the business is restocked of all or nearly all goods and merchandise damaged and/or destroyed by the covered loss. Obviously, the cost of the goods being restocked is paid by the commercial property policy (CPP) and not the business income protection; but the time it takes to restock is included as part of the period of restoration.

However, the point at which a manufacturing operation is considered restocked differs from the point at which a non-manufacturing operation is restocked. Manufacturing operations are restocked once they arrive at the same level of raw stock and goods in process existing prior to the loss. Non-manufacturing operations are not considered restocked until they are at the same level of inventory available for sale or use as existed prior to the loss.

The definition of Extended Business Income highlights the difference between the entity types. Extended business income, per the policy, "*begins on the date property (except 'finished stock') is actually repaired, rebuilt or replaced and 'operations' are resumed....*" "Finished stock" is defined, in part, to mean "*stock you have manufactured.*"

Combine these two policy provisions and it becomes evident that the time required to return to the level of finished stock (stock manufactured by the insured) on hand is not part of the period of restoration. This is a reasonable limitation as the insured was paid for the finished stock under the commercial property policy and any extension of time necessary to replace the finished stock would in essence result in double payment (once for the property and again for additional lost time).

By extrapolation the business income form excludes from the calculation of the period of restoration and the business income loss the time required to replace finished stock, but this exclusion is more evident in the cause of loss form. ISO's Special Cause of Loss Form (CP 10 30) specifically states in 4.a.(1) (b) *"We will not pay for any loss caused by or resulting from the time required to reproduce 'finished stock.'"*

If the finished stock was sold but not yet delivered, the CPP pays the selling price (less discounts and expenses); a type of business income protection. Stock not yet sold is valued at cost (unless the Manufacturer's Selling Price endorsement (CP 99 30) is attached), so the insured has already been paid to build a replacement (even if valued at actual cash value (ACV)).

This step should theoretically add no time to the period of restoration for non-manufacturing operations as arrangements should have been made during all the preceding steps to have the necessary goods ready to stock the operation immediately upon receiving a certificate of occupancy (CO).

Manufacturing operations may likely see additional time added to the period of restoration since the time to restock includes the time necessary to return to the level of goods in process existing prior to the loss. The amount of additional time is based on two factors: 1) the availability of production machinery; and 2) the length of the manufacturing process.

Hiring, Rehiring and Training

Only employers that choose to exclude or limit payroll by use of the CP 15 10 should be subject to this time factor. Employers that keep all employees on the payroll during the period of restoration have no need to hire, rehire, or train, as they still have the same group of trained employees.

However, this is a non-factor in regard to the insurable period of restoration. If the employer chooses to limit or exclude payroll of any employees, extending the period of restoration to allow time to rehire or train these employees would violate the intent of the CP 15 10.

While hiring, rehiring, and training may have to be done, the employer/insured does so on its own time, not the insurance carrier's time.

Replacement of Production Machinery

Returning to operational capability means that a manufacturing operation must have the machinery and equipment necessary to resume production at the same level that existed prior to the loss. This does not mean that the insured will produce the same amount of goods; it just means it is able to produce at pre-loss levels.

When estimating the period of restoration, the time required locating, purchasing, installing, and testing replacement production machinery must be considered. The period of restoration does not end until each of these steps is accomplished. After all, a brand-new building without production equipment is nearly as useless as a building reduced to rubble. The purpose of the building is to house the equipment that makes the goods which are sold to generate revenue/profit.

To reduce this to its simplest terms, the building makes no money for the insured; the equipment does. Until the equipment is in place and operational, no money can be made, and the insured is still out of business.

If all the steps necessary to rebuild the building can be accomplished in nine months but replacement equipment cannot be available for 12 months, the period of restoration is 12 months, the resulting coinsurance choice is 100%, and 100% of the developed business income exposure is purchased.

A client was convinced that his building could be rebuilt in six months. He was going to purchase half the 12-month business income and use a 50% coinsurance percentage until one last question was posed: "How long will it take to get your production machinery?" The insured stated that would take a minimum of nine months because much of the equipment was custom-made.

The insured chose to increase the business income coverage and coinsurance amount to account for the additional time period. The moral of the story is to estimate the period of restoration based on the time required to replace what generates the revenue, not just the building that houses that equipment.

Building Codes Are Bad

Of the 10 factors controlling an entity's return to full operational capability, governmental involvement may have the most detrimental effect. Ordinances and laws often skew the estimated rebuilding schedule and extend the time the operation is or could be shut down.

Unendorsed time element forms specifically exclude from the defined period of restoration any increase in time directly attributable to government intervention, further complicating the calculation of the eligible business income loss. ISO's definition of "period of restoration" reads as follows.

> *"Period of restoration" does not include any increased period required due to the enforcement of any ordinance or law that:*
> *(1) Regulates the construction, use or repair, or requires the tearing down, of any property; or*
> *(2) Requires any insured or others to test for, monitor, clean up, remove, contain, treat, detoxify or neutralize, or in any way respond to, or assess the effects of "pollutants."*

Throughout this chapter, a worst-case-scenario loss has been assumed. The same assumption applies to ordinance or law losses. The structure's failure to meet a jurisdiction's ordinances or laws could turn what is only a partial loss into a worst-case-scenario total loss just by the existence of building codes. Understanding this increase-in-loss scenario necessitates an awareness of all issues surrounding ordinances and laws — collectively, the "building codes" (as they are referred to for the remainder of this chapter) to which the building is subject.

Source of Building Codes

Building codes are enforced by local jurisdictions but are promulgated by an assortment of contributors. Local jurisdictions, state governments, and the federal government each add something to jurisdictionally-enforced building codes.

The vast majority of building and building-products-related codes are promulgated by advisory organizations, such as the International Building Code Council (IBC) and the National Fire Protection Association (NFPA). A 1996 study conducted by the National Institute of Standards and Technology (NIST) found that more than 93,000 codes established by more than 700 advisory organizations apply to construction products and methods. Luckily only a relatively small number of these codes actually apply to the structure itself (most of these codes relate to the materials used in construction).

When Governments Get Involved

Specific legal requirements stipulate the point at which a structure must be brought into compliance with local building codes. Existing structures are usually "grandfathered" and are not required to immediately comply with current building codes unless certain statutorily-specified events occur. "Major structural damage" is one of those qualifying events.

Major structural damage (major damage) does not offer a universal definition; each jurisdiction establishes and applies its own interpretation of the term. There are, however, two broad major damage categories into which most state and local building codes fall.

- ***The Jurisdictional Authority Rule***: States using this as the measure of major damage allow the authority having jurisdiction (the local government) to decide when a damaged building must be brought into compliance with current building codes.
- ***The Percentage Rule***: States and jurisdictions applying this rule require a building damaged beyond a certain percentage of its "value" or square footage (the rarest option) be brought, in its entirety, into compliance with local building codes.

Both rules present unique problems. The jurisdictional authority rule is subjective in its application; and the definition of "value" differs among the states that apply the percentage rule. Knowing which major damage rule applies is of utmost importance when planning for the "building code" contingency in the period of restoration.

How This Extends the Period of Restoration

Regardless of which rule is subscribed to by a particular jurisdiction, building code violations have the potential to turn a partial loss into a functional total loss, greatly extending the time required to return to full operational capability (the period of restoration).

Assume, for example, the insured structure is located in a jurisdiction subscribing to the percentage rule. Any structure damaged beyond 50% of its value must be brought into full compliance with current building codes. Bringing the building up to code may require demolition of the undamaged portion of the building and complete reconstruction of the entire building.

Assume a building sustains fire damage equal to 60% of its value on June 1. If the insured is allowed by the jurisdiction to use the existing structure and simply rebuild the damaged section, the building could be completed, retooled, and restocked by December 1 (six months). However, because the damage exceeds the building code's percentage threshold, the entire building must be brought into full compliance with the current building codes. To accomplish that, the undamaged part of the building must be torn down and the entire structure rebuilt. As a result, the building does not return to operational capability until March 1, nine months after the loss.

Based on the definition of "period of restoration" found in the unendorsed policy, the three additional months of lost income is excluded from coverage. Any income lost due directly to the application of building codes is paid out of the insured's own pocket. Without the proper endorsements, this could be quite an expensive gap.

Of course, no building-code-related loss can be pinpointed or proven this easily, by either side. This is but an example to spotlight the incredibly expensive effect of building codes. The additional work and time required to bring a damaged building into compliance with current building codes is a function of several factors.

- The building codes to which the structure is subject.
- Which "rule," as discussed above, to which the building is subject.
- How far "out of compliance" the building is.
- The political climate and speed of action (how quickly can or will a decision be rendered).
- Any special or unusual regulations or laws to which the entity is subject (i.e., the EPA, historical societies, etc.).

Estimating the additional time required to return the business to operational capability because of the adverse application of building codes is impossible. The only good news is that the insured does not have to know or delineate which building codes to which the structure is subject.

Ordinance or Law - Increased Period of Restoration (CP 15 31)

To redefine the period of restoration to include the increased period of operational suspension caused by or resulting from the enforcement of any building code in force at the time of the loss requires attachment of the Ordinance or

Law – Increased Period of Restoration (CP 15 31) to the policy. No time limit applies to the endorsement. Any additional loss of income directly related to the application of the jurisdiction's building codes is paid by the insurance carrier, provided adequate limits have been purchased.

Attaching the CP 15 31 requires the insured to adjust the period of restoration, coinsurance, and limit of coverage to account for the additional time period covered by the endorsed policy. The coinsurance penalty is not altered by the attachment of the endorsement, so all limits and amounts must reflect the estimated increase in time.

A highlight of the coverage extension is that it indemnifies the insured income lost while the building is being rebuilt to meet all applicable building codes. This includes building codes related to losses not generally covered in the commercial property forms provided the damage leading to the enforcement of the building code is caused by a covered cause of loss. Flood damage is a prime example.

Flood damage is nearly always excluded in ISO property forms. However, structures located in special flood hazard areas (SFHAs) are required to meet specific flood plain management regulations unless "grandfathered." Should that structure suffer damage from a covered cause of loss sufficient to cross the FEMA threshold amount (FEMA's definition of the threshold amount is outside the scope of this book), the building must be brought into compliance with current flood plain management requirements. Although flood damage is not covered by the policy, the CP 15 31 pays the additional loss of income sustained while the building is being brought into compliance with the flood-related building codes.

There is no limitation as to which building codes are covered by the endorsement. The form specifically covers "any" ordinance or law affecting the structure.

Importance of the CP 15 31

If business income is the most important coverage the insured can have (as was postulated in the first chapter), the CP 15 31 is one of the most important business income endorsements.

Most buildings in some way fail to meet current building codes. Age has a lot to do with that, but so, too, does the number and breadth of building code changes since the building was constructed and/or renovated. Any building more than five years old should have the CP 15 31 endorsement, and it is almost a requirement on any building more than 10 years old.

How much time might the application of the building codes add to the period of restoration? They could add three months or six months, there is no way to know. But without the endorsement (available to all three time element forms), any additional loss of income as a result of building codes would come out of the insured's own financial resources.

(An in-depth study of Ordinance or Law coverage is found in the book, *"Wow! I Never Knew That! 12 of the Most Misunderstood and Misused P&C Insurance Coverages, Concepts and Exclusions."*)

The Period of Restoration

Correctly estimating the period of restoration directly affects the development of the coinsurance percentage (detailed in Chapter 6) which relates specifically to the coverage limits purchased (detailed in Chapter 7). The period of restoration is the key to the Time Doctrine, the business income coverage limit, and the business income coverage concept.

Chapter 6
Calculating Coinsurance

Commercial property coinsurance is based almost exclusively on the property values at risk. Did the insured carry adequate limits compared to the values present (based on the valuation method chosen)? No other factor or information is necessary.

In contrast, the amount of income at risk is secondary to develop the business income coinsurance. In fact, it is not even a requirement. Business income's coinsurance percentage can be estimated and decided upon before the CP 15 15 worksheet is ever completed. In short, the amount subject to loss has no bearing on the coinsurance percentage. In fact, the estimated amount subject to loss is a function of the coinsurance percentage (the exact opposite of the property coverage). This may sound like insurance heresy.

Business income coinsurance is solely a function of time, a 12-month period of time to be more specific. How long will it take, following a worst-case-scenario loss, to return the operation to pre-loss conditions and capabilities (operational capability)? This is the period of restoration as detailed in Chapter 5. Knowing the period of restoration allows the insured to accomplish two tasks: 1) pick the correct coinsurance; and 2) decide on the minimum limit of business income coverage to purchase. Again, the ultimate amount subject to loss and the coinsurance percentage are both a function of the period of restoration.

Coinsurance is not necessary to develop the coverage limit, but it is used to calculate the coverage limit. Its function is to assure that the insured purchases a specified minimum limit of coverage so that the insurance carrier collects ample premium for the risk being written. This is the same purpose coinsurance has in property coverage.

What the Percentages Mean

ISO-published coinsurance percentages are 50, 60, 70, 80, 90, 100, and 125%. Some carriers have filed proprietary coinsurance percentages as high as 150%. Each percentage represents a proportion of one year. For a point of reference, here are the coinsurance equivalents in relation to 12 months.

- 50 percent = 6 months
- 60 percent = 7.2 months
- 70 percent = 8.4 months
- 80 percent = 9.6 months
- 90 percent = 10.8 months
- 100 percent = 12 months
- 125 percent = 15 months

If the insured believes it can return to operational capability following a worst-case-scenario loss in six months or less, it uses 50% coinsurance and purchases at least 50% of the 12-month business income exposure developed by the CP 15

15. The choice of a particular coinsurance percentage is based on the estimated period of restoration.

On the other end of the spectrum, if the insured believes two years will be required to return to operational capability following a worst-case-scenario loss it chooses 125% coinsurance (the maximum available from ISO) and purchases two times the 12-month BI exposure developed by the CP 15 15. (Note: the coinsurance percentage does not limit the length of payout.)

When considering coinsurance percentages and limits, the higher the coinsurance percentage, the lower the rate per $100 of coverage. But never increase the coinsurance percentage without a corresponding increase in limits due to the coinsurance penalty. Increasing limits solely to garner a higher coinsurance percentage may backfire at the time of a loss. Other options are presented in Chapter 7.

Business Income Coinsurance Examples

Time is intrinsic to the development of business income coinsurance and ultimately the choice of coverage limits. Two exhibits are attached for ease of review: 1) Exhibit 6.1 is a sample of a completed business income report/worksheet (CP 15 15); and 2) Exhibit 6.2 provides several coinsurance calculation examples applying the data from the sample worksheet (Exhibit 6.1). The two primary formulas used in these exhibits are the "maximum coinsurance percentage calculation" and the "estimated loss of income (amount subject to loss) calculation".

- **Maximum Coinsurance Percentage Calculation**: Number of months required to accomplish the four period of restoration objectives/12 (the number of months in a year) = Maximum Coinsurance Percentage
  Use of the term "maximum coinsurance percentage" is intentional to remind insureds and agents of potential coinsurance penalties for underestimating the upcoming policy year (remember, the next 12 months are being insured, not the previous 12). Use the amount of coverage developed by applying the maximum coinsurance percentage to the 12-month exposure but apply the next lowest coinsurance percentage in the policy if the developed percentage falls in between available options.

- **Estimated Loss of Income (Amount Subject to Loss) Calculation**: Maximum Coinsurance Percentage x 12 months business income calculation (J.1. or J.2. amount) = Amount Subject to Loss

The amount of business income purchased can and usually does match the calculated "amount subject to loss" or be slightly higher, but it should certainly never be lower. Two occasions may necessitate the need for the insured to purchase a higher business income limit than the developed "amount subject to loss".

1. The calculated maximum coinsurance percentage falls between available options (see example 3 in Exhibit 6.2). Should that occur, the insured can either: a) raise

the limit purchased to match the next higher coinsurance number with a corresponding coinsurance increase; or b) purchase the developed amount subject to loss but lower the coinsurance percentage to the next available lower level (never lower the coverage limit).

2.   When the insured is not positive about the estimates for the upcoming year. (An option to manage this situation is the attachment of the Business Income Premium Adjustment endorsement (CP 15 20) which makes the BI form a reporting form).

Picking the preferred amount of business income coverage is more specifically detailed in Chapter 7.

It Really Is That Easy

Calculating the business income coinsurance has been incorrectly taught for so long that this explanation may seem too simple; it's not. Calculating coinsurance really is this easy and simple; it's estimating the period of restoration leading to the correct choice of the maximum coinsurance percentage that is difficult (as is detailed in Chapter 4).

Some insurance educators and texts claim that the coinsurance calculation in some way involves the use of the insureds gross sales; it doesn't. Both the policy wording and the business income report/worksheet are explicit that certain expenses do not apply to either the calculation of the 12-month business income, or to the calculation of the coinsurance percentage or its penalty. Anyone that says otherwise is ignoring the forms.

This is called "time element" coverage for a reason; it is based on time. What is the minimum amount of time required to return the business to full operational capability? That is all the information necessary to estimate the period of restoration and develop the maximum coinsurance percentage.

Exhibit 6.1(1)

POLICY NUMBER: **COMMERCIAL PROPERTY**
                                                  CP 15 15 10 12

BUSINESS INCOME REPORT/WORKSHEET

Date: Today	
Your Name	**Location**
Your Best Insured	123 As Always Main Street My Town, American City 98765

This worksheet must be completed on an **accrual** basis.

The beginning and ending inventories in all calculations should be based on the same valuation method.

Applicable When The Agreed Value Coverage Option Applies:
I certify that this is a true and correct report of values as required under this policy for the periods indicated and that the Agreed Value for the period of coverage is $, based on a Co-insurance percentage of   %.
Signature: **Official Title:**

Applicable When The Premium Adjustment Form Applies:
I certify that this is a true and correct report of values as required under this policy for the 12 months ended: **Signature:**   **Official Title:**   **Agent Or Broker:**   **Mailing Address:**

Exhibit 6.1(2)

BUSINESS INCOME REPORT/WORKSHEET
FINANCIAL ANALYSIS

Income And Expenses	12 Month Period Ending 12/31/2013		Estimated For 12 Month Period Beginning 1/1/2014	
	Manufacturing	Non-Manufacturing	Manufacturing	Non-Manufacturing
A. Gross Sales	$ 2,000,000	$	$ 2,250,000	$
B. Deduct: Finished Stock Inventory (at sales value) At Beginning	- 500,000		- 650,000	
C. Add: Finished Stock Inventory (at sales value) At End	+ 650,000		+ 700,000	
D. Gross Sales Value Of Production	$ 2,150,000		$ 2,300,000	
E. Deduct:				
Prepaid Freight – Outgoing	- 20,000	-	- 22,000	-
Returns And Allowances	- 100,000	-	- 108,000	-
Discounts	- 50,000	-	- 54,000	-
Bad Debts	- 80,000	-	- 86,000	-
Collection Expenses	- 20,000	-	- 22,000	-
F. Net Sales		$		$
- Net Sales Value Of Production	$ 1,880,000		$ 2,008,000	
G. Add:				
Other Earnings From Your Business Operations (not investment income or rents from other properties):				
Commissions Or Rents	+	+	+	+
Cash Discounts Received	+	+	+	+
Other	+	+	+	+
H. Total Revenues	$ 1,880,000	$	$ 2,008,000	$

Exhibit 6.1(3)

Income And Expenses	12 Month Period Ending 12/31/2013		Estimated for 12 Month Period Beginning 1/1/2014	
	Manufacturing	Non-Manufacturing	Manufacturing	Non-Manufacturing
Total Revenues (Line H. from previous page)	**$ 1,880,000**	**$**	**$ 2,080,000**	**$**
I. Deduct:				
Cost Of Goods Sold (See page 5 for instructions.)	- 575,000	-	- 600,000	-
Cost Of Services Purchased From Outsiders (not your employees) To Resell, That Do Not Continue Under Contract	- 75,000	-	- 80,000	-
Power, Heat And Refrigeration Expenses That Do Not Continue Under Contract (if CP 15 11 is attached)	- 20,000		- 25,000	
All Payroll Expenses Or The Amount Of Payroll Expense Excluded (if CP 15 10 is attached)	-	-	-	-
Special Deductions For Mining Properties (See page 6 for instructions.)	-	-	-	-
J.1. Business Income Exposure For 12 Months	**$ 1,210,000**	**$**	**$ 1,303,000**	**$**
J.2. Combined (firms engaged in manufacturing and non-manufacturing operations)	$		$	
The Figures In J.1. Or J.2. Represent 100% Of Your Actual And Estimated Business Income Exposure For 12 Months.				

Exhibit 6.1(4)

Income And Expenses	12 Month Period Ending: 12/31/2013		Estimated for 12 Month Period Beginning: 1/1/2014	
	Manufacturing	Non-Manufacturing	Manufacturing	Non-Manufacturing
K. Additional Expenses:				
1. Extra Expenses – Form CP 00 30 Only (expenses incurred to avoid or minimize suspension of business and to continue operations)			$	$
2. Extended Business Income and Extended Period Of Indemnity – Form CP 00 30 Or CP 00 32 (loss of Business Income following resumption of operations for up to 60 days or the number of days selected under Extended Period Of Indemnity option)				
3. Combined (all amounts in K.1. and K.2.)			+	+
			$ 1,303,000	

                                  "Estimated" Column

L. Total Of **J.** And **K.** $

The figure in L. represents 100% of your estimated Business Income exposure for 12 months, and additional expenses. Using this figure as information, determine the approximate amount of insurance needed based on your evaluation of the number of months needed (may exceed 12 months) to replace your property, resume operations and restore the business to the condition that would have existed if no property damage had occurred.

Refer to the agent or company for information on available coinsurance levels and indemnity options. The Limit of Insurance you select will be shown in the Declarations of the policy.

Exhibit 6.1(5)

Supplementary Information				
	12-Month Period Ending: 12/31/2013		Estimated for 12-Month Period Beginning: 1/1/2014	
Calculation Of Cost Of Goods Sold	Manufacturing	Non-Manufacturing	Manufacturing	Non-Manufacturing
Inventory At Beginning Of Year (including raw material and stock in process, but not finished stock, for manufacturing risks)	$ 400,000	$	$ 425,000	$
Add: The Following Purchase Costs: Cost Of Raw Stock (including transportation charges)	+ 450,000		+ 500,000	
Cost Of Factory Supplies Consumed	+ 100,000		+ 130,000	
Cost Of Merchandise Sold Including Transportation Charges (for manufacturing risks, means cost of merchandise sold but not manufactured by you)	+ 15,000	+	+ 20,000	+
Cost Of Other Supplies Consumed (including transportation charges)	+ 35,000	+	+ 50,000	+
Cost Of Goods Available For Sale	$ 1,000,000	$	$ 1,125,000	$
Deduct: Inventory At End Of Year (including raw material and stock in process, but not finished stock, for manufacturing risks)	- 425,000	-	- 525,000	-
Cost Of Goods Sold (Enter this figure in Item **I.** on page 3.)	$ 575,000	$	$ 600,000	$

Exhibit 6.1(6)

Supplementary Information		
Calculation Of Special Deductions - Mining Properties		
	12-Month Period Ending:	Estimated for 12-Month Period Beginning:
Royalties, Unless Specifically Included In Coverage	$	$
Actual Depletion, Commonly Known As Unit Or Cost Depletion (not percentage depletion)	+	+
Welfare And Retirement Fund Charges Based On Tonnage	+	+
Hired Trucks	+	+
Enter This Figure In Item **I.** On Page 3.	$	$

© **Insurance Services Office, Inc.**

Exhibit 6.2

Business Income Coinsurance Examples	
Business Income Exposure for 12 Months (Taken from J.1. on sample worksheet – Exhibit 6.1)	$1,303,000
"Maximum Coinsurance Percentage"	Estimated Period of Restoration / 12
"Estimated Loss of Income"	Maximum Coinsurance Percentage x 12-month Business Income Exposure
Example 1:	
Estimated "Period of Restoration"	12 months
Maximum Coinsurance Percentage (12/12)=	100%
"Estimated Loss of Income"	$1,303,000 (Amount Subject to Loss)
Minimum BI Limit Purchased	$1,303,000
Example 2:	
Estimated "Period of Restoration"	6 months
Maximum Coinsurance Percentage (6/12)=	50%
"Estimated Loss of Income"	$651,500 (Amount Subject to Loss)
Minimum BI Limit Purchased	$651,500
Example 3:	
Estimated "Period of Restoration"	9 months
Maximum Coinsurance Percentage (9/12)=	75% (Apply this percentage to the 12-month exposure, but use 70% on the policy)
"Estimated Loss of Income"	$977,250 (at 75%) (Amount Subject to Loss)
Minimum BI Limit Purchased	$977,250
Example 4:	
Estimated "Period of Restoration"	15 months
Maximum Coinsurance Percentage (15/12)=	125%
"Estimated Loss of Income"	$1,628,750 (Amount Subject to Loss)
Minimum BI Limit Purchased	$1,628,750

Term Descriptions:

"Period of Restoration": The total time required to: 1) rebuild or find an alternate location; 2) replace equipment; 3) restock/replenish; and 4) return to previous level of operational capability/capacity." External factors may lengthen the "period of restoration" beyond the time period covered by the unendorsed business income policy. These factors affecting these objectives and correcting endorsements are detailed in Chapter 5.

"Maximum Coinsurance Percentage": The estimated "period of restoration" divided by 12 months.

"Estimated Loss of Income" and *"Minimum BI Limit Purchased"*: To avoid a coinsurance penalty, these figures should generally match or the Business Income limit should be slightly higher than the estimated loss of income; especially if the calculated coinsurance falls in between available limits (as in Example 3). The *"estimated loss of income"* is also known as *"Amount Subject to Loss."* Detailed in Chapter 7.

Chapter 7
Calculating the Correct Amount of Business Income Coverage

Business income's developed coinsurance percentage, as detailed in Chapter 6, is primarily a function of time. The maximum coinsurance percentage is developed based on the amount of time reasonably expected to complete the four prime objectives of the period of restoration as detailed in Chapter 5, compared against a one-year basis period:

$$\text{Estimated Period of Restoration}/12 = \text{Maximum Coinsurance Percentage}$$

Although time is the basis for the coinsurance calculation, the unendorsed/unaltered business income policy settles claims based on the limits purchased. Likewise, any applicable coinsurance penalty is calculated by comparing the amount of business income purchased (insured) with the estimated 12-month business income exposure (as calculated in the CP 15 15) multiplied by the chosen coinsurance percentage.

(Did/Should) X Loss = Ultimate BI Payment

- **Did**: The amount of business income insurance actually purchased.
- **Should**: The estimated 12-month business income exposure (taken from J.1.) multiplied by the coinsurance percentage chosen as a result of the

legitimate estimation of the worst-case period of restoration (either the maximum coinsurance percentage or something lower).

- **Loss**: Compensable business income (not the same as insurable income) lost during the period of restoration.

Correctly calculating the proper amount of business income coverage requires the insured to apply all the information discussed thus far in this book. An accurate business income limit calculation depends on the legitimate estimation of the worst-case period of restoration.

Estimating the legitimate worst-case period of restoration necessitates understanding the time required to accomplish each step in the period of restoration process. Only by applying this "time doctrine" to business income can the correct business income coverage limit be chosen.

All business income losses are settled based on the limit of coverage, but the limit cannot be determined without proper application of the "time doctrine." [1] Again, business income coverage is called time element coverage for a reason.

A Word About 'Should'

Developing "should" to apply to the business income coinsurance calculation is direct and simple. Should is the estimated 12-month business income exposure (the J.1. amount) multiplied by (X) the coinsurance percentage chosen by the insured.

Some suggest that "should" is developed by adding the insured's net income to all usual and customary operating expenses then multiplying that total by the chosen coinsurance percentage. This would be true if and only if it wasn't for the second half of the coinsurance condition. Many texts and instructors seem to ignore this particular section of the business income form. So this incorrectly taught method of developing "should" is nothing more than wrong.

The business income coverage form specifically deducts certain operating expenses from the "*total of all operating expenses*" when applying the coinsurance condition. A copy of the business income coinsurance condition is found in Exhibit 7.1. Pay particular attention to the deductions listed at the end of the condition. Note that both the business income coverage form and the Business Income Report/Worksheet (CP 15 15) subtract the same expenses from the operating costs (with only minor differences in the cost of goods sold).

Essentially, the same figures are used to develop J.1. (or J.2.) and the "should" used in calculating the business income coinsurance penalty. That is proof once again that business income coverage is fundamentally a time-based coverage and has nothing to do with gross earnings or even total operating cost.

How the Coinsurance Percentage Applies to Payout

Coinsurance percentages do not limit the amount of time for which business income coverage is provided. The business income policy pays all loss of business income, as the term is defined in the policy, until 1) the limits of coverage are gone; or 2) the point at which the insured should have reasonably been able to return to operational capability is reached; whichever occurs first. (Both statements assume coverage amounts sufficient to avoid a coinsurance penalty.)

To demonstrate, ISO's maximum coinsurance percentage is 125%, but the maximum period of restoration is not capped at 15 months. If 18 months are required to return to operational capability, the policy covers the entire amount/period provided there are adequate limits. The 125% only relates to the application of the coinsurance penalty. This same concept is true of any chosen coinsurance percentage.

As long as 1) business income is being lost; 2) coverage limits are available; and 3) the insured could not reasonably have been expected to return to operational capability, the business income policy continues to pay. In short, business income coverage written on a coinsurance basis is an actual loss sustained coverage.

That makes the coinsurance percentage somewhat less important than assumed and puts the emphasis back on the coverage limit chosen. The primary concern is that the insured carries limits high enough to get through the entire estimated worst-case period of restoration. Coinsurance is secondary in the order of importance. With an accurate estimation of the period of restoration leading to adequate coverage limits, coinsurance becomes a non-factor, provided the time doctrine is followed.

Avoiding a Coinsurance Penalty

Coinsurance, in all property coverages, is nothing more than the method employed by insurance carriers to force the insured to purchase limits that accurately reflect the exposure. The threat of a coinsurance penalty allows the insurer to receive a fair, exposure-based premium.

Because the insured receives the lesser of A) the limit of coverage purchased; or B) the reduced amount of coverage resulting from the application of a coinsurance penalty, the insured must plan accordingly when purchasing business income protection. Insureds may choose to do one or both of these.

1. Purchase a coverage limit high enough to avoid a coinsurance penalty.
2. Apply a coinsurance percentage lower than what the coverage amount/limit represents.

Ether option avoids a coinsurance penalty, but only the first assures ample coverage should the covered period of restoration be longer than expected. Neither of these options requires an endorsement to the policy. There is a third option for avoiding a coinsurance penalty, but it does require the attachment of an endorsement; the CP 15 20 (this option is discussed later in the chapter).

Option 1 - Ample Limits of Protection

When the insured legitimately and accurately assesses the period of restoration, calculating the amount of coverage should be straightforward and easy. But remember, the chosen business income limit must represent the expected income for the upcoming policy period.

To avoid underestimations and a potential coinsurance penalty, the insured may consider applying a "gap factor" to the business income amount developed using the previously provided formula.

> 12-month business income exposure (developed from the CP 15 15) multiplied by the Maximum Coinsurance Percentage = Business Income Limit.

This gap factor option may be necessary to account for any unexpected increase in revenue and/or to provide a cushion against an unexpectedly long period of restoration.

Option 2 - Lower the Coinsurance Percentage

Because the coinsurance percentage does not act to limit the amount of time the business income loss is paid, purchasing the business income limit developed by applying the maximum coinsurance percentage but lowering the applicable coinsurance percentage is a second option for avoiding the possibility of a coinsurance penalty.

Insureds choosing option 2 must resist any temptation to lower the coverage limits developed applying the maximum coinsurance percentage (MCP) to the 12-month business income exposure. The coverage limit developed using the MCP represents the insured's likely actual loss of business income. Lowering the coinsurance percentage is intended solely to avoid a possible coinsurance penalty; it does not serve as a reason to lower the business income limit. Never lower the coverage limit.

This is the preferred option when the developed MCP falls in between available options.

A Third Option

The third option for avoiding coinsurance incorporates the use of option 1 (using a gap factor to increase limits) and attaching an endorsement to the business income coverage form – the Business Income Premium Adjustment endorsement (CP 15 20).

Essentially the business income coverage form becomes an annual reporting form with the attachment of this endorsement. The initial premium is based on the BI limit developed at the beginning of the policy period (taken from the CP 15 15-derived BI amount) multiplied by the coinsurance percentage chosen by the insured. The final premium is derived from the actual business income (J.1) calculated at the end of the policy period multiplied by the applicable coinsurance percentage.

At the end of the policy period, the insured submits a revised business income report showing actual figures for the prior policy period rather than merely estimates. The reports are due within 120 days of the end of the policy period. If the reported business income limit is higher than the initial estimate, the insurance carrier bills for the additional premium. If the reported BI is lower than the initial estimate, the insured receives a return premium.

The endorsement states that the insured shall never be paid more than the policy limit. Although this is a reporting-type form, the insured must still have adequate policy limits in place at the time of the loss to cover the income lost during the entire period of restoration, and to avoid a coinsurance penalty. There is also a penalty assessed if a report has not been turned in to the carrier as prescribed in the policy; its calculation is similar to a coinsurance calculation.

Insureds with unpredictable year-to-year business income fluctuations may be the best candidates for this endorsement. Any insured using this endorsement should estimate high (paying an initially higher premium) then take advantage of the reporting procedure to adjust the premium to the actual exposure. The insured should be fully covered following a worst-case-scenario loss, yet always end the year paying the exactly correct premium because of the reporting procedure.

Note that this endorsement option cannot be coupled with the Agreed Value non-coinsurance option (detailed in Chapter 10); nor can this be used with two of the dependent property endorsements: 1) the Business Income From Dependent Properties – Broad Form (CP 15 08); or 2) the Business Income From Dependent Properties – Limited Form (CP 15 09). Both endorsements are detailed in Chapter 12.

A Worksheet

Business income coverage, because of its extreme importance, requires simplification. Thus far this book has attempted to clarify business income but may have served only to intensify the fear and confusion surrounding coinsurance, the period of restoration, and how to choose the proper limits. To ease this tension, a simplified worksheet incorporating all the information discussed in Chapters 4 to 7 into two pages (a cheat sheet, so to speak) is provided.

In fact, two worksheets follow this chapter. The first is a completed worksheet (Exhibit 7.2) allowing the user to see how it works. The second is a blank worksheet (Exhibit 7.3) that can be used to develop the correct coinsurance, period of restoration, and business income limits.

The worksheet is dependent on the accurate completion of the CP 15 15 (Business Income Report/Worksheet). Without a correct CP 15 15, the calculator is little help beyond providing the maximum coinsurance percentage.

[1] **Time Doctrine** – All business income losses are settled based on the coverage limit purchased. An accurate business income coverage limit calculation depends on an accurate estimation of the 12-month business income exposure and the legitimate estimation of the worst-case period of restoration. Estimating the worst-case period of restoration necessitates understanding the time required to accomplish each of the 10 steps within the four period of restoration objectives. The key to business income is the correct estimation of time.

Disclaimer: *Wells Media Group, Inc. (including previous entities, subsequent entities, subsidiary entities or family of operations) does not guarantee that use of this form accounts for all period of restoration factors. This calculator is just one tool that can be used to assist in estimating business income. Individual risks require individual attention. The duty to assess an insured's exposures lies solely with the insured and/or the agent or broker.*

Exhibit 7.1

ISO's Business Income Coinsurance Condition:

D. Additional Condition

COINSURANCE

If a Coinsurance percentage is shown in the Declarations, the following condition applies in addition to the Common Policy Conditions and the Commercial Property Conditions.

We will not pay the full amount of any Business Income loss if the Limit of Insurance for Business Income is less than:

    1. The Coinsurance percentage shown for Business Income in the Declarations; times

    2. The sum of:

        a. The Net Income (Net Profit or Loss before income taxes), and

        b. Operating expenses, including payroll expenses, that would have been earned or incurred (had no loss occurred) by your "operations" at the described premises for the 12 months following the inception, or last previous anniversary date, of this policy (whichever is later).

Instead, we will determine the most we will pay using the following steps:

    Step **(1):** Multiply the Net Income and operating expense for the 12 months following the inception, or last previous anniversary date, of this policy by the Coinsurance percentage;

    Step **(2):** Divide the Limit of Insurance for the described premises by the figure determined in Step **(1);** and

    Step **(3):** Multiply the total amount of loss by the figure determined in Step **(2).**

We will pay the amount determined in Step **(3)** or the limit of insurance, whichever is less. For the remainder, you will either have to rely on other insurance or absorb the loss yourself.

In determining operating expenses for the purpose of applying the Coinsurance condition, the following expenses, if applicable, shall be deducted from the total of all operating expenses:

(1) Prepaid freight – outgoing;

(2) Returns and allowances;

(3) Discounts;

(4) Bad debts;

(5) Collection expenses;

(6) Cost of raw stock and factory supplies consumed (including transportation charges);

(7) Cost of merchandise sold (including transportation charges);

(8) Cost of other supplies consumed (including transportation charges);

(9) Cost of services purchased from outsiders (not employees) to resell, that do not continue under contract;

(10) Power, heat and refrigeration expenses that do not continue under contract (if Form CP 15 11 is attached);

(11) All payroll expenses or the amount of payroll expense excluded (if Form CP 15 10 is attached); and

(12) Special deductions for mining properties (royalties unless specifically included in coverage; actual depletion commonly known as unit or cost depletion – not percentage depletion; welfare and retirement fund charges based on tonnage; hired trucks).

Exhibit 7.2(1)

NAMED INSURED:	Your Best Insured	
ENTITY TYPE:	Manufacturing	
AGE OF BUILDING:	15 years	
12-Month Business Income Amount (J.1.):	$1,375,000	

	Activity Days	Chargeable Days
Property Loss Adjustment Process [A]		60
Pre-construction Activities		
Building plans drawn, reviewed, & approved:	75	
General Contractor found & hired:	30	
Apply for and receive building permit:	14	
Schedule & perform site clearance/ preparation:	21	
Total Activity Days (TAD):	140	
Chargeable Activity Days (TAD x 35%)[B]		49
Construction Time [C]		160
Chargeable Days Subtotal (CDST) = A+B+C		269
Post Construction Duties (add to CDST)		
Add 15% for Manufacturing Operations		40
Add 5% for Non-Manufacturing Operations		
Age of Building Factor (Add to CDST)		
Add 5% if over 10 years old	13	
Add 10% if over 25 years old		
Miscellaneous Construction Time Factors (CDST x 5%)		13
Total Estimated Perion of Restoration (TEPOR) in days		335
Maximum Coinsurance Percentage (TEPOR/365)		92%
Amount Subject to Loss		$1,265,000
(12 mo. BI x Maximum Coinsurance Percentage)		
Coinsurance Chosen (Next higher or next lower)		90%
Limit Chosen (increase limit to match coinsurance)		$1,265,000

Exhibit 7.2(2)

Work Sheet Instructions and Descriptions

Amount of 12-month Business Income: This is taken directly from "J.1." or "J.2." of the completed Business Income Report/Worksheet (CP 15 15). Remember, this is the upcoming 12-month estimate.

Property Loss Adjustment Process: First step in the Period of Restoration. May take longer than expected. See prior article detailing this process.

Pre-Construction-Related Activities: Much of these activities can be completed during the adjustment process and thus are not necessarily linear. Only 35% of the Total Activity Days (TAD) are considered chargeable. This results in the Chargeable Activity Days.

Construction Time: This estimate should account for all construction-related activities (exterior and interior) and include time for any unforeseen events. This period will be a function of the age, size, complexity and other factors surrounding the structure.

Chargeable Day Subtotal: This is the total of the Property Loss Adjustment Process, the Pre-Construction Chargeable Activity Days and the Construction Time.

Post-Construction Duties include the time necessary to restock, rehire and replace production machinery and equipment (if applicable). Timing necessary to complete these duties may differ based on the entity type. Manufacturing operations add 10% to the Chargeable Day Sub-Total (CDST) and non-manufacturing entities add 5% to the CDST.

Age of Building Factor: Older buildings may require extra time to rebuild due to the application of an ordinance or law. Buildings over 10 years old are assigned an additional 5% (CDST x 5%).

Miscellaneous Construction Time Factors: Weather, economic conditions, etc. may lengthen the time it takes to rebuild. A minimum of 5% additional time should be added to the CDST to account for these unknowns. (CDST x 5%).

Total Estimated Period of Restoration (TEPOR): CDST + Post-Construction Duties + Age of Building Factor + Miscellaneous Construction Time Factors = TEPOR. This is used to develop the "Maximum Coinsurance Percentage" and the estimated amount of Business Income subject to loss.

Maximum Coinsurance Percentage: TEPOR/365. This represents the maximum coinsurance percentage the insured should consider using on the policy. If this percentage falls between two acceptable options, the insured can: 1) Increase the coinsurance to the next higher available amount, with a corresponding increase in the limit with a "gap factor;" or 2) Lower the coinsurance percentage to the next lowest acceptable amount WITHOUT lowering the limit of coverage developed.

Amount Subject to Loss: Amount of 12-month Business Income (above) multiplied by the maximum coinsurance percentage. This is the expected loss of income based on the estimated Period of Restoration.

Exhibit 7.3(1)

NAMED INSURED: _____

ENTITY TYPE: Manufacturing Non-Manufacturing

AGE OF BUILDING: ___ Years

12-Month Business Income Amount (J.1.): [_____]

Chargeable Days

Property Loss Adjustment Process [A]

Pre-Construction Activities

Activity Days

Building plans drawn, reviewed & approved: _____

General Contractor found and hired: _____

Apply for and receive building permit: _____

Schedule & performs site clearance / preparation: _____

Total Activity Days (TAD)

Chargeable Activity Days (TAD x 35%)[B] _____

Construction Time [C] _____

Chargeable Days Sub-Total (CDST) = A+B+C [_____]

Post Construction Duties (Add to CDST)

If a Manufacturing Operation – Add 15%: _____

If a Non-Manufacturing Operation – Add 5%: _____

Age of Building Factor (Add to CDST)

Add 5% if over 10 years old / 10% if over 25 years old _____

Miscellaneous Construction Time Factors (CDST x 5%) _____

Total Estimated Period of Restoration (TEPOR) in days [_____]

Maximum Coinsurance Percentage (TEPOR / 365)

Amount Subject to Loss (12 mo. BI x Maximum Coinsurance Percentage:

Coinsurance Chosen (Increase to next highest or decrease to next lower)

[_____]

Limit Chosen (If increase coinsurance, must increase limit) [_____]

Exhibit 7.3(2)

Work Sheet Instructions and Descriptions

Amount of 12-month Business Income: This is taken directly from "J.1." or "J.2." of the completed Business Income Report/Worksheet (CP 15 15). Remember, this is the upcoming 12-month estimate.

Property Loss Adjustment Process: First step in the Period of Restoration. May take longer than expected. See prior article detailing this process.

Pre-Construction-Related Activities: Much of these activities can be completed during the adjustment process and thus are not necessarily linear. Only 35% of the Total Activity Days (TAD) are considered chargeable. This results in the Chargeable Activity Days.

Construction Time: This estimate should account for all construction-related activities (exterior and interior) and include time for any unforeseen events. This period will be a function of the age, size, complexity and other factors surrounding the structure.

Chargeable Day Subtotal: This is the total of the Property Loss Adjustment Process, the Pre-Construction Chargeable Activity Days and the Construction Time.

Post-Construction Duties include the time necessary to restock, rehire and replace production machinery and equipment (if applicable). Timing necessary to complete these duties may differ based on the entity type. Manufacturing operations add 10% to the Chargeable Day Sub-Total (CDST) and non-manufacturing entities add 5% to the CDST.

Age of Building Factor: Older buildings may require extra time to rebuild due to the application of an ordinance or law. Buildings over 10 years old are assigned an additional 5% (CDST x 5%).

Miscellaneous Construction Time Factors: Weather, economic conditions, etc. may lengthen the time it takes to rebuild. A minimum of 5% additional time should be added to the CDST to account for these unknowns. (CDST x 5%).

Total Estimated Period of Restoration (TEPOR): CDST + Post-Construction Duties + Age of Building Factor + Miscellaneous Construction Time Factors = TEPOR. This is used to develop the "Maximum Coinsurance Percentage" and the estimated amount of Business Income subject to loss.

Maximum Coinsurance Percentage: TEPOR/365. This represents the maximum coinsurance percentage the insured should consider using on the policy. If this percentage falls between two acceptable options, the insured can: 1) Increase the coinsurance to the next higher available amount, with a corresponding increase in the limit with a "gap factor;" or 2) Lower the coinsurance percentage to the next lowest acceptable amount WITHOUT lowering the limit of coverage developed.

Amount Subject to Loss: Amount of 12-month Business Income (above) multiplied by the maximum coinsurance percentage. This is the expected loss of income based on the estimated Period of Restoration.

Chapter 8

When Business Income Is Lost After Reopening - Extended Business Income

Arriving at the end of the defined period of restoration does not generally trigger the insured's immediate return to pre-loss operational income levels. The ability to generate revenues at the same level enjoyed prior to the suspension of operations may require several weeks or months following the insured's return to operational capability (the ability to operate at pre-loss levels).

During the period of restoration, the insured's customers and clients may find alternate sources for the goods, services, or products the insured provides. In so doing, those customers may develop new buying habits or enter into a replacement contractual relationship with another entity. Regaining those customers and the revenue they represent takes time. Replacing prior customers and clients with new buyers requires even more time.

Both business income coverage forms (CP 00 30 and CP 00 32) provide a small amount of automatic coverage to indemnify the insured for the income/revenue lag experienced once operations are resumed. Additional coverage **5.c. Extended Business Income** historically provided 30 days of difference in income coverage following the insured's return to operational capability. In 2013, this additional coverage was extended to 60 days following the entity's return to operational capability.

How Does the Coverage Extension Apply?

Extended Business Income protection is divided into two parts. Part c. (1) extends business income to policies covering *Business Income other than Rental Value.* Part c. (2) provides the same protection but to policies protecting against the loss of *Rental Value.* Rental Value is covered whether it is included as part of the business income protection or provided on a stand-alone basis.

Extended protection for *Business Income other than Rental Value* begins upon the resumption of the entity's operations. Coverage ends: 1) when the insured is generating the same amount of business income that would have been earned had no loss occurred; or 2) in 60 consecutive days; whichever occurs first.

Likewise, *Rental Value* protection commences *on the date property is actually repaired, rebuilt, or replaced and tenantability is restored.* Coverage ceases when the tenant occupancy could be restored to pre-loss levels, or in 60 consecutive days following tenantability, whichever comes first.

Note that Extended Business Income protection does not allow and is not designed to help the insured recover income lost due to externally poor economic conditions present following the insured's return to operational capability. If the insured's ability to return to pre-loss income levels is stunted by the surrounding community's economic condition, the coverage extension does not apply.

For example, assume an insured is located in an area devastated by a hurricane. Six months following the damage, the insured is able to return to operational capability. However, the remainder of the business community and its residents are unable to return for several more months, causing the insured major income loss. The loss of income attributable to this lack of customer base does not qualify as a business income loss under the coverage extension.

How Much Will the Insured Be Paid During the Extension?

Both business income forms (CP 00 30 and CP 00 32) state that under the extended business income provision the insured is paid the amount of business income lost between the resumption of operational capability and the earliest of: 1) the return to its pre-loss operational income level; or 2) 60 consecutive days.

Presumably, some income is earned during the extension period, but likely not as much as would have been earned had no business-closing loss occurred. Calculating the extended business income amount requires knowing (or estimating) both revenue levels. The insured is paid the difference between the business income that would have been earned had no loss occurred and the actual business income earned during the extension period.

Remember, business income is *the net profit or loss before tax that would have been earned had no loss occurred plus continuing normal operating expenses.* During the defined period of restoration (business shut down or slow down), there is likely no or only minimal revenue, and the normal operating expenses are reduced as per the term "continuing." Once full operational capability is reached, income levels increase, to some extent, and there is also an increase in operating expenses. Some expenses that were lowered or discontinued during the business shut-down are reestablished upon resumption of operations.

Basically, the unaltered business income coverage form pays for up to 60 additional days following the business' return to operational capability (subject to the policy's coverage limits). However, this period and its representative amount of business income is not part of the period of restoration and is not used in the application or calculation of any coinsurance penalty.

Does the Insured Need to Increase the Business Income Limit?

Extended business income limits are not in addition to the limit of business income coverage purchased. The income lost during the extended period is paid out of the business income limit purchased. However, the insured does not necessarily need to increase the coverage amount to fund the 60-day extension.

The expense section of Chapter 4 clarified that it is not necessary for the insured to know or even consider which operating expenses will or will not continue, nor at what level any of those expenses will continue, following a business-closing loss. Non-continuing sales and production-related expenses are the only expenses subtracted from gross sales (or gross sales value of production) when completing the business income report/worksheet (CP 15 15). All other operating expenses are included in the insurable/ratable business income exposure (the J.1 or J.2. total), not just those that continue during the period of restoration.

Insurable business income, as developed by the CP 15 15, is actually greater than the payable (compensable) business income; theoretically leaving the insured some level of coverage limit to cover at least part of the 60 additional days of protection, especially if a gap factor is used. Thus, the business income limit may need only a slight increase to provide the 60 days of additional protection, provided the period of restoration was correctly estimated initially.

Continuing Versus Non-Continuing Expenses Related to Extended Business Income

Many operational expenses are reduced or disappear completely during the period of restoration. However, the insured is not charged with deciphering which operational expenses will be affected by any business-closing loss.

No hard rule or method exists to gauge the difference between pre-loss operational expenses and the operating expenses likely to continue during the period of restoration. Much of the difference depends on the endorsements used (i.e., the payroll limitation or exclusion) and the nature of the operation.

Even a 20% difference between pre-loss operational expenses and continuing operating expenses during the period of restoration generates a wide gap between the insured and compensable amount of business income. See Exhibit 8.1 at the end of the chapter.

The difference between the insurable business income and the payable business income in the exhibit is $200,000. Applying the information in the referenced example, $226,027 is required to pay the 60-day extension. Some income should be realized once operations resume, so it is unlikely that the entire surplus amount will be required to cover these 60 days of extended business income. There may not be a need to increase the business income limit, provided, again, the period of restoration was correctly estimated. (Warning: The 20% is for example purposes only and not intended to be used as a guide or rule. Depending on the operation, the difference between insurable and compensable could be more or less requiring a review on the need to account for this period of payment.)

Explaining the difference between insurable and compensable business income is the goal of Chapter 9. Here is a warning in preparation for the upcoming discussion: Do not consider lowering the business income limit due to the insurable/compensable difference; the coinsurance condition prevents such action.

What If 60 Days Is Not Enough?

Insureds have the option to increase the time and limit of extended business income coverage if the automatic 60-day extension is insufficient. By simply activating the Extended Period of Indemnity optional coverage on the declarations page, picking a limit, and paying an additional premium, the insured can increase the time limit in various increments up to a maximum of 730 days. Available increments are: 90, 120, 150, 180, 270, 365, 450, 540, 630, and 730 days.

If the insured decides to increase the time span of coverage, it must decide how much additional coverage is needed (beyond 60 days); and place this amount in the K.2. line of the Business Income Report/Worksheet (CP 15 15).

Calculating the necessary amount of additional coverage needed is surprisingly simple. First, the insured divides the J.1. (or J.2. if applicable) amount by 365 and multiplies the product by the number of days coverage is needed beyond the original 60 days. If the insured believes 180 days (six months) of coverage is required and his J.1. amount is $1.375 million; the additional amount of coverage is developed as follows:

$$(\$1,375,000/365) \times (180-60) = K.2.$$
$$\$3767.12 \times 120 = \$452,055$$

Remember, the product does not need to be multiplied by 180 days as the insured already has 60 days of coverage granted by the form. Only the additional days need be calculated.

But why use the full J.1. amount in this calculation rather than some percentage of that total? Because the insured is assuming a crippling loss of income during this extended period plus the operational expenses return to pre-loss levels even if/though the revenue stream doesn't (making all expenses "continuing normal operating expenses"). The insured may not need the full limit purchased, but over-insured is better than underinsured.

This amount is transferred over to K.2. on page 4 of the CP 15 15. Once the extra expense limit in K.1. is added (as discussed in Chapter 11), the CP 15 15 is complete.

How Much Additional Coverage

The answer to how much additional extended business income protection might be needed is truly a function of the insured. Different operations likely require very different extended periods of indemnity.

- Retail operations may require the shortest amount of time to return to pre-loss income levels. The extended period of indemnity required may only be 30 to 60 days.
- Restaurants and other like operations might require four to six months (120 to 180 days) to return to pre-loss income levels.
- Hotels could require six months to one year (180 to 365 days) because of event contracts, etc. Of course, this depends on the operation.
- Manufacturing operations, depending on the type, etc., could reasonably require more than a year to return to pre-loss income levels.

Exhibit 8.1

Extended Period of Indemnity BI Example	
Business Income Exposure for 12 Months (Taken from J.1. on sample worksheet)	$1,375,000
"Maximum Coinsurance Percentage"	Estimated Period of Restoration / 12
"Estimated Loss of Income"	Maximum Coinsurance Percentage x 12-month Business Income Exposure ("J.1." or "J.2.")
Estimated **"Period of Restoration"**	12 months
Insurable/Ratable Business Income	
Maximum Coinsurance Percentage	100%
Minimum BI Limit Purchased	$1,375,000
Operating Expense Information	
All Normal Operating Expenses (ANOE) – Prior to a loss	$1,000,000
Continuing Normal Operating Expenses (CNOE) – Following a Loss	$800,000
Extended Period of Indemnity (60 days)	
Amount of Business Income Coverage Available (ANOE – CNOE)	$200,000
Estimated Maximum 60-Day Extended Business Income Loss ((Limit of BI Purchased/Days in Period of Restoration) x 60)	$226,027

Term Descriptions:

"Period of Restoration": The "Period of Restoration" represents the total time it takes for the insured to: 1) rebuild or find an alternate location; 2) replace equipment; 3) restock/replenish; and 4) return to previous level of operational capability/capacity." External factors may lengthen the "period of restoration" beyond the time period covered by the unendorsed business income policy.

"Days in Period of Restoration": This is the estimated period of restoration converted to days. In this example, the estimated period of restoration is 1 year (12 months) which translates to 365 days.

"Maximum Coinsurance Percentage": Business income coinsurance is based initially on a 12-month time span, developing the maximum coinsurance percentage simply requires the estimated "period of restoration" be divided by 12.

"Minimum BI Limit Purchased": The "estimated loss of income" is also known as "Amount Subject to Loss."

"All Normal Operating Expenses" (ANOE): These are the insured's operating expenditures that would be made during normal operation had no loss occurred.

"Continuing Normal Operating Expenses" (CNOE): These are the operating expenses that continue during the "Period of Restoration."

Chapter 9
Insurable Versus Compensable Business Income

Insurable business income is the amount used to calculate the business income premium (the J.1. (or J.2.) total multiplied by the maximum coinsurance percentage based off the estimated worst-case period of restoration). This amount includes all of an entity's operating expenses with the exception of a few specific non-continuing sales-related and production-related expenses detailed in Chapter 4. And it does not matter when developing insurable business income whether any other non-contemplated expenses continue, are reduced, or disappear during the period of restoration.

Compensable business income is the actual amount of business income paid to cover the amount of income lost during the period of restoration. It is the amount necessary to indemnify the insured. Compensable business income is some amount less than the insurable business income because it is based on net profit or loss before tax plus actual ongoing (continuing) operating expenses incurred during the period of restoration. This represents the amount arrived at when all reduced or discontinued operating expenses are subtracted to produce the continuing normal operating expenses.

Nearly every chapter to this point has concentrated on calculating and applying the insurable business income developed by the Business Income Report/Worksheet (CP 15 15); and Chapter 8 briefly mentioned the difference between insurable and compensable business income. However, this chapter focuses on the actual amount the insured can expect to be paid following a covered, business-closing loss, the compensable business income amount.

Business Income Defined - Once Again

ISO's two business income coverage forms (CP 00 30 and CP 00 32) define business income as follows:

Business Income means the:

a. *Net Income (Net Profit or Loss before income taxes) that would have been earned or incurred; and*

b. *Continuing normal operating expenses incurred, including payroll.*

Applying this definition and the amount it represents, the insurance carrier agrees to indemnify the insured for its actual loss of business income suffered during the period of restoration. If all coinsurance conditions are met, the only limit on protection is the limit of coverage purchased.

Compensable business income complies with the indemnification concept by returning the insured to the same financial condition that existed prior to the loss or, in the case of business income protection, would have existed had no loss occurred. But the amount necessary to indemnify the insured does not equate to the amount of insurance purchased because the method for calculating the 12-month business income exposure differs from the method for calculating the business income loss.

The 12-Month Business Income Exposure

Chapter 4 was dedicated to the development of the 12-month business income exposure (the J.1. or J.2. amount); there is little need to recap that discussion. At this point, it is sufficient to mention that only two classes of expenses are considered and deducted when developing the insured's business income exposure: sales-related expenses and production-related expenses.

Sales-related expenses are deducted from gross sales (or gross sales value of production) to produce the insured's "Total Revenues" (line H of the CP 15 15). Those expenses are incurred or potentially incurred following the sale of a product or service and include the following.

- Prepaid freight – outgoing
- Returns and allowances
- Discounts
- Bad debts
- Collection expenses

Production-related expenses are subtracted from Total Revenues, leaving the 12-month business income exposure (J.1. or J.2.). Production-related expenses represent the cost of buying or building the products/services being sold to the customer and include the following.

- Cost of goods sold (Note: not calculated according to GAAP standards)
- Cost of services purchased from outsiders to be resold that do not continue under contract
- Power, heat and refrigeration expenses that do not continue (if CP 15 11 is attached)
- Excluded payroll expenses (if CP 15 10 is attached)
- Special deductions for mining operations (if the insured is a mining operation only)

Only those expenses are deducted when completing the business income report/worksheet. Because of this, the 12-month insurable business income total is always going to be more than the compensable business income amount, except, possibly when a loss exceeds the contemplated worst-case scenario.

What's the Difference?

Estimating the difference between the insurable business income exposure (J.1.) and the compensable business income exposure is nearly impossible. Prior to the loss there is no way to accurately guess how much of which expenses will continue, be reduced, or disappear; and it really doesn't matter.

Recognizing that there is a difference between insurable and compensable business income is important if for no other reason than to be able to explain the difference to the insured. Disappointment and dissatisfaction are a function of expectation. If the insured expects more than he is due, that's where the problem lies.

When Might the Difference Be Noticeable?

Any business income loss may serve to highlight the difference between insurable and compensable business income, but such difference is more likely noticeable when there is a partial insured-period loss. For example, consider an insured who estimates a 12-month, worst-case-scenario period of restoration. The insured purchases $100,000 in business income protection at 100% coinsurance (due to the estimated 12 months of down time) to cover his 12-month, J.1. total. (Yes, it is a small number, but this amount is used for ease of calculation and for the sake of the example).

Fire damage results in the insured being shut down for six months. By interpolation, the insured expects to receive $50,000 ($100,000 x 50%). But because 30% of the normal operating expenses ceased during the shutdown, the insured's compensable business income loss totaled only $40,000 (The business income form covers net profit plus continuing normal operating expense so 70% of the entire amount cannot be used in this example). The additional $10,000 is not required to indemnify the insured for the lost net income plus the operating expenses that continued during the business' closure.

Remember, indemnification requires only that the insurance carrier pay for (indemnify) the lost profit plus the continuing operating expenses during the period of restoration (the actual loss sustained). Paying any more would improve the insured's position and violate the principle of indemnification.

What Can Be Done to Adjust for this Difference?

Nothing! Nothing can be done about the difference between insurable and compensable business income due to the application of the coinsurance penalty. The business income coinsurance penalty is calculated by applying the same deductions used to develop the 12-month business income exposure in the CP 15 15.

Lowering the limit of coverage to account for the difference between the insurable and compensable amount does nothing but subject the insured to a coinsurance penalty and possible under-insurance. Chapters 4 and 7 listed the only deductions that apply to the calculation of the coinsurance penalty. Non-continuing operating expenses are not deducted nor considered in the coinsurance condition.

Some suggest lowering the business income limit and applying a correlating reduction in the coinsurance percentage. As mentioned in Chapter 7, the higher rate associated with lower coinsurance percentages largely negates any perceived gains from such an action. The lower coverage could end up costing more.

The insured should do nothing to adjust for the difference. There is, however, a benefit that flows from the difference between insurable and compensable business income.

The Benefit

Additional coverage limits are built into the business income protection as a result of the difference between the insurable business income amount and the compensable business income amount. Because of the difference, the insured is protected for its 60 days of extended business income protection with little need to increase the limit (see Chapter 8). Plus, some limits may be available should the period of restoration run longer than expected.

The insured is not simply paying for coverage that will never be used, the difference actually acts as a safety net for the insured. Remember, the only limit on business income loss payment is the amount of coverage available as long as: 1) there is no coinsurance penalty being applied; 2) the period of restoration is within what is considered reasonably expected; and 3) no other exclusions apply (i.e. the application of an ordinance or law). If these conditions are met, the actual business income loss sustained is covered until the limit is exhausted.

Chapter 10
Three Non-Coinsurance Business Income Options

Three non-coinsurance options are available for the insured's use if the prospect of calculating the business income limit using the CP 15 15 and/or explaining coinsurance still causes concern. Two options completely remove coinsurance from the picture, and one simply suspends the application of coinsurance for one year.

- Business Income Agreed Value
- Monthly Limit of Indemnity
- Maximum Period of Indemnity

Business Income Agreed Value

Business income agreed value suspends the coinsurance condition for 12 months. Qualifying for agreed value protection still requires the insured to complete the Business Income Report/Worksheet (CP 15 15) at the beginning of the policy period and every year thereafter. If an updated worksheet is not completed annually, the policy reverts back to a coinsurance form with all its applicable penalties; so, this is not the best option if the insured (or the agent) is trying to avoid the worksheet.

Not only is the insured required to complete the worksheet, but an officer or other responsible party must also sign and attest to the information on the worksheet specifying: 1) the value the insured has agreed to carry; and 2) the desired coinsurance percentage. So, this is not the best non-coinsurance option if the insured is trying to avoid the worksheet.

Agreed value signifies that the insured and the underwriter agree upfront on the amount of insurable business income subject to loss. The insured agrees to carry that pre-determined amount of coverage. In return, the underwriter agrees to pay the entire business income loss up to that limit without the application or consideration of coinsurance.

To clarify, the insured is not required to carry nor is it limited to the 12-month business income amount calculated using the worksheet. The amount purchased is and should be based on the estimated period of restoration and the percentage of a year that period represents. Calculating the period of restoration and ultimately the coinsurance is still necessary as detailed in earlier chapters. All ISO-published coinsurance percentages are available for use with the agreed value option (50, 60, 70, 80, 90, 100 and 125%).

For an easy example, assume the insured estimated that a full 12 months is required to return to operational capability and selects 100% coinsurance (estimated period of restoration / 12 = maximum coinsurance percentage) to account for the estimated time. If the insured chooses the business income agreed value option with 100% coinsurance, he is now committed to purchasing the full 12-month business income estimated amount (J.1.). If the insured purchases any amount less than the required calculated amount, he is subject to a loss payment penalty.

The agreed value loss-payment penalty is calculated exactly like the coinsurance penalty, except that it has nothing to do with the miscalculation of the actual business income during the coverage period. The penalty is assessed because the insured failed to purchase the amount of coverage needed, and the underwriter agreed would and should be in place. In essence, the insured is penalized for not meeting contractual requirements, whereas the traditional coinsurance penalty is assessed to assure the insured carries proper coverage and that the insured collects ample premium for the exposure.

Exhibit 10.1 demonstrates the difference between business income agreed value and traditional coinsurance. For sake of the example, assume the insured is a manufacturing operation that underestimated the actual business income earned during the coverage period (period of restoration). All the necessary information for the calculation and comparison is found in the example.

Without the agreed value option, the insured could have been out-of-pocket more than $61,000. How much greater would the uninsured amount have been had this been a much larger manufacturing entity? Hundreds of thousands of dollars could be left for the insured to pay.

Business income agreed value is a useful coinsurance-suspending option. Because the insured and the underwriter agree to the exposure and coverage amounts in advance, there is no question whether there is enough coverage at the time of the loss. Only a total shutdown exceeding the estimated maximum period of restoration shows the effects of any business income underestimation.

Activating this option increases the business income premium by approximately 10% compared to the traditional coinsurance coverage. However, business income agreed value has the lowest rate per $100 of protection of the three non-coinsurance options presented in this chapter.

As stated in an earlier chapter, the agreed value option cannot be combined with the business income premium adjustment endorsement (CP 15 20).

Monthly Limit of Indemnity

This option to traditional coinsurance-based coverage allows the insured to avoid coinsurance completely and sidestep the requirement of completing a business income report/worksheet. There is no real upfront calculation associated with this option. The only calculation done is at the time of the loss, to decipher the maximum limit available during any one 30-day period.

Two decisions are required of the insured when this option is chosen: 1) the limit of coverage; and 2) the monthly limit of indemnity coverage fraction. No "formal" income calculations are done, so the limit is little more than a guess made by the insured. The second decision requires the insured to choose from among the three available monthly limit fractions: one-third (1/3), one-fourth (1/4), and one-sixth (1/6).

The monthly limit fraction serves to cap the amount of coverage available in any 30-day period. The chosen amount of coverage is multiplied by the fraction to arrive at the maximum payout during each 30-day period. For instance, if the insured purchases $300,000 of coverage, the maximum amount available in any 30-day period is as shown.

- 1/3 monthly limit = $100,000 maximum available for each 30-day period
- 1/4 monthly limit = $75,000 maximum available for each 30-day period
- 1/6 monthly limit = $50,000 maximum available for each 30-day period

One myth surrounding the Monthly Limit of Indemnity option is the function of the denominator in claims settlement and payout. Some believe, and even teach, that the denominator (the bottom number) limits the number of months the insured gets paid. That is, if the insured chooses a 1/3-monthly limit of indemnity, coverage is only provided for three months. This is fully and completely false, unless the limits are completely used in the first three months.

The denominator serves no other purpose than to limit the amount the insured can receive in any one 30-day period. Continuing with the above example, if the insured chooses the 1/3 monthly limit of indemnity, it has up to $100,000 available for any 30-day period during the period of restoration. Business income loss payments continue until the insured uses up the full $300,000 or returns to full operational capability, whichever comes first. If it takes six months to use up the entire $300,000, that's how long the policy pays.

Monthly limit of indemnity, contrary to its name, is actually a non-indemnity option, meaning that the amount of coverage has no real or known relationship to the insured's business income exposure or estimated period of restoration. As such, the insured is entitled to receive the entire amount regardless of how long it takes. Again, the only two limitations are: 1) the monthly limit (as decided by the fraction); and 2) a return to operational capability before the limits are completely used.

If coverage is provided using the CP 00 30 (Business Income (and Extra Expense) Coverage Form), it is important to remember that the fraction does not apply to the extra expense coverage. However, the amount needed to cover any extra expense must be added to the business income limit purchased.

For example, if the insured wants $300,000 business income (BI) coverage and $120,000 extra expense (EE) coverage, it should purchase $420,000 in total protection. The maximum payout is limited to $420,000, but the amount available for extra expense in any one month is not limited by the fractional amount. If the 30-day BI amount exceeds the fractional limit, the entire extra expense loss is still paid. This payout process continues until the total of both BI and EE losses reaches the limit purchased.

See Exhibit 10.2 for a demonstration of the monthly limit of indemnity loss settlement with extra expense coverage (using the CP 00 30). The example assumes $420,000 and the 1/6-monthly limit of indemnity. Notice that the payout goes beyond six months paying until the limit is exhausted.

Maximum Period of Indemnity

The last and simplest of the non-coinsurance options is the maximum period of indemnity. This option limits business income and extra expense payments to 120 days, until the limit is spent, or the insured returns to operational capability, whichever occurs first. Like the monthly limit of indemnity, the amount of business income purchased is little more than a guess.

This is a good option only if there is absolutely no question that the insured can return to operational capability within 120 days. Insureds that qualify might include those with these characteristics.

- They do not require any specialized facilities to operate and can run the business from practically any location. These insureds do not own the building and have quick access to leasable space.
- They can operate using other locations to absorb the production lost at the damaged facility (this is probably rare).

Maximum period of indemnity is a non-indemnity option. Like the monthly limit of indemnity option, the limit of coverage is not based on the actual exposure. Unlike the monthly limit option, coverage is limited to a specific number of days. If the insured does not use the entire limit during the 120-day period, the insured is simply out of luck (to some extent as he still had his business income exposure paid during the 120 days).

Of the three non-coinsurance options, the maximum period of indemnity option carries the highest rate. Of course, the higher rate is somewhat offset by the lower limits likely purchased.

Why Are These Options Necessary?

With the detailed discussion of the CP 15 15 in earlier chapters, looking for a non-coinsurance option out of lack of understanding should no longer be necessary. However, if an insured is unsure of the amount of expected business income or is unwilling to provide the required accounting data, a non-coinsurance option that does not require the completion of the CP 15 15 may be the only way to cover the business income exposure.

Exhibit 10.1

Agreed Value vs. Traditional Coinsurance Loss Payment Calculation	
Estimated 12-Month Business Income Exposure (BI Exp.)	$1,375,000 ("J.1.")
Estimated **"Period of Restoration"** (POR)	12 Months
"Maximum Coinsurance Percentage" (MCP) (MCP = POR/12) (Remember, all coinsurance options are available)	100%
"Estimated Loss of Income" / **Agreed Amount** (BI Exp. x MCP)	$1,375,000
ACTUAL 12-month Business Income (based on all relevant financial data at the time of the loss)	$1,620,000
Loss from 3-month shutdown (based on actual)	$405,000
Coinsurance Calculations	
Traditional Coinsurance Calculation (Calculated using the actual business income)	Amount of BI Purchased (**DID**) Actual BI x Coinsurance % (**SHOULD**)
Agreed Value Calculation (Calculated applying the "agreed" upon business income)	Amount of BI Purchased (**DID**) **BI Agreed Amount** x Coinsurance % (**SHOULD**)
Traditional Coinsurance Loss Payment Calculation	
Amount of Business Income Purchased (DID)	$1,375,000
Actual Amount of Business Income (SHOULD)	$1,620,000
Calculation	DID/SHOULD x LOSS = Payment (($1,375/$1,620) x $405,000)
Amount of Payment	**$343,750**
Uninsured Amount (Due to Coinsurance Penalty)	$61,250

Business Income Agreed Value Loss Payment Calculation	
Amount of Business Income Purchased (DID)	$1,375,000
Business Income Agreed Value (SHOULD)	$1,375,000
Calculation	DID/SHOULD x LOSS = Payment (($1,375/$1,375) x $405,000)
Amount of Payment	**$405,000**
Uninsured Amount	None – **Loss is Fully Covered**

Exhibit 10.2

Monthly Limit of Indemnity Example	
Business Income Limit (**BI**)	$300,000
Extra Expense Limit (**EE**) (Only available if the CP 00 30 is used)	$120,000
Total Limit (**TL**) (BI+EE=TL)	$420,000
Monthly Limit of Indemnity (**MLI**)	1/6
Maximum **Business Income** each 30 Days (TL x MLI)	$70,000

Example Using Above Data				
Month	**Business Income Loss**	**Extra Expense Loss**	**Total Paid in Month**	**Running Total**
#1	$60,000	$10,000	$70,000	$70,000
#2	$75,000	$5,000	$75,000	$145,000
#3	$90,000	$10,000	$80,000	$225,000
#4	$80,000	$10,000	$80,000	$305,000
#5	$50,000	$5,000	$55,000	$360,000
#6	$30,000	$5,000	$35,000	$395,000
#7	$25,000	$5,000	$25,000 (all that is left)	$420,000
#8	$20,000	$10,000	NONE (limit used up)	$420,000

Chapter 11

Extra Expense Coverage -
With or Without Business Income

Two ISO time element forms provide extra expense protection: the *Business Income (and Extra Expense) Coverage Form* (CP 00 30); and the *Extra Expense Coverage Form* (CP 00 50). The CP 00 30 requires the insured to select an amount of coverage to be paid in addition to the business income amount. The CP 00 50, as the form name suggests, provides only extra expense protection. Both forms require the desired amount of extra expense coverage to be specifically scheduled.

Essentially the same definition of extra expense is used in both forms. And with only one minor variation, each calculates the eligible loss payment by applying the same parameters. The one difference between the forms is the method for distributing the coverage limits following a covered loss event.

Expenses Covered

Maintaining at least partial operational continuity following a major property loss is the goal of extra expense coverage. Conceptually and theoretically, if some income can be produced, the overall cost of the business income claim is likely to be lower, even with the additional expenses necessary to setup and maintain operations in an alternate location.

Secondary to the goal of producing some level of income is simply the continuance of operations, even partially. Businesses, like individuals, tend to take longer to return to full, pre-loss operational levels once they become sedentary compared to those that remain active. Overall, the period of restoration may be shorter if some activity is continued.

Operational continuity, as the term suggests, means that the business continues to operate and produce some amount of goods or services following a loss-induced business suspension. While production is not likely to equal or even approach pre-loss levels, the insurance carrier's desire is to encourage some level of continued operations at the insured premises or at a temporary alternate location.

To accomplish some level of operational continuity, extra expense coverage pays the necessary additional expenses incurred during the period of restoration that would not have been incurred had no loss occurred (paraphrase of ISO wording) by paying expenses such as these.

1. The additional costs necessary to speed-up real property repairs to avoid or minimize the suspension of operations at the insured location (if possible).

2. The cost to relocate to another location either temporarily or permanently to avoid or minimize the suspension of operations. Additional costs may include: facility rental costs, utility hook-ups, furniture and equipment rental costs, advertising costs, etc. (if the new location is permanent, the period of restoration ends).

3. Any increased operating costs related to a new, temporary location.

4. Expediting expenses necessary to speed the replacement of machinery, equipment, or other business personal property.

Reducing the amount of business income loss is not necessarily a prerequisite for the insured to be paid for the incurred extra expenses. Relocation and additional operating expenses (2. and 3. above) are reimbursable even if the incurrence of such costs does nothing to lower the business income loss. However expediting expenses, the additional cost necessary to replace or repair real or business personal property (including machinery or equipment), are only considered a covered extra expense to the extent that such expense reduces the business income loss.

For example, assume the insured suffers a fire that destroys a piece of machinery that is absolutely essential to its operation. The supplier of the machine states that it can replace the destroyed equipment in 12 months. The insured cannot operate without this piece of machinery so, for a 10% up-charge, the manufacturer agrees to expedite the manufacture and delivery of the machine, guaranteeing its delivery in nine months. The additional cost to expedite the delivery is a covered extra expense to the extent that it shortens the "period of restoration" and lowers the business income loss.

But if 10 months are required to rebuild the structure, only a percentage of the expediting cost is considered eligible extra expense. The reason is the machine's expeditious return shorted the "period of restoration" by only two months (12 months potential minus 10 months actual) rather than three (12 months potential minus 9 months potential).

These same provisions apply to both the CP 00 30 and the CP 00 50.

Limitations on Extra Expense Payments

Both the CP 00 30 and the CP 00 50 forms require the insured to choose a specific extra expense limit. However, the two forms diverge regarding the method of loss payment. The CP 00 30 does not delineate nor restrict how the extra expense limit is distributed, but the CP 00 50 rations the extra expense limit based on a pre-chosen formula.

The *Business Income (and Extra Expense) Coverage Form* (CP 00 30) allows the insured to spend the extra expense limit in as short or long a time period as it takes to use the limit. The only two CP 00 30 limitations are the limit of coverage and the period of restoration. The insured chooses a limit (mostly just a guess) and places it on Line K.1. of the business income report/worksheet found on page 4 (this is the last blank, every line of the CP 15 15 has been detailed). The insured can spend the entire extra expense limit in the first 10 days following the loss or spread over six months, the policy pays either way. However, no extra expense loss is paid once the period of restoration ends. And unlike business income, there is no extended extra expense coverage.

Pure extra expense coverage provided by the *Extra Expense Coverage Form* (CP 00 50) follows a payout schedule chosen by the insured at policy inception. The insured chooses one of three standard payout options and indicates the choice on the time element supplemental application (ACORD 810). Following a loss, the specified limit is incrementally available as prescribed by the indicated payout percentage option. These are the three standard options.

A. 100% - 100% - 100% (the most expensive of the three options)

B. 40% - 80% - 100% (the most frequently chosen option)

C. 35%-70%-100% (the least expensive of the available

ISO's CLM Rule 53 allows for three non-standard options when the CP 15 07 (*Expanded Limits on Loss Payment*) is attached to the Extra Expense form:

30%-60%-90%-100%
25%-50%-75%-100%
20%-40%-80%-100%

options)

Each percentage represents the total amount of coverage available during each 30-day period. For instance, option A allows the insured to access the entire amount of extra expense coverage immediately following the loss. (Option A does not mean that the insured has access to three times the limit purchased.)

Contrast option A with options B and C, which limit the amount of coverage available in the first 30 and 60 days following the loss. From the 61st day forward, the insured has access to the entire limit. The percentages represent the maximum amount available at the end of each 30-day period.

Using option B to demonstrate the rolling total/maximum amount concept, assume an extra expense limit of $100,000. During the first 30 days, the insured has up to $40,000 available to cover extra expenses. At the end of 60 days, the insured could have spent up to $80,000 (but the payout during the second 30 days is not limited to $40,000 unless the full $40,000 was used in the first 30 days). From 61 days forward, the insured can access the full $100,000 — however long it takes (subject to the return to full operational capability). Look at this example.

- Extra Expenses during first 30 days: $20,000
- Amount Paid: $20,000
- Extra Expenses during 31-60 days: $60,000
- Amount Paid: $60,000 ($80,000 total)
- Extra Expenses after 60 days: $30,000
- Amount Paid: $20,000 ($100,000 total)

The above example demonstrates the rolling total, maximum amount concept. The insured is not limited to just $40,000 in the second 30 days unless the full amount allowable in the first 30 days was completely spent. Because the insured suffered extra expenses of only $20,000 during the first 30 days, the difference between 80% of $100,000 and the amount of extra expense already paid ($20,000) was available during the second 30-day period.

This same breakdown and rolling total concept apply to each option.

Who Needs Extra Expense Protection?

Some operations, such as banks, newspapers, insurance agencies, contractors, and other like entities, cannot afford to be shut down for any length of time; they need to be operational as quickly as possible following a loss. Extra expense coverage is essential for these operations. Such entities may suffer only minor business income loss, but the expense required to stay in business and operational at the same or alternate location could be high.

Businesses that need to be operational quickly are the targets for extra expense coverage. Deciding whether extra expense should be coupled with business income protection is based on the insured's business, availability of alternate locations, and the estimated time required to return to operational capability at an alternate location (if at all possible). Some businesses can operate anywhere and can be operational within a couple of days. They don't necessarily need business income coverage (since there is a 72-hour time deductible) and may only require pure extra expense coverage. However, most businesses that can benefit from extra expense coverage also need some business income coverage, especially those dependent on a specific location, space requirements, or specialized machinery or equipment.

Pricing Extra Expense Coverage

An interesting fact: *Business Income (with Extra Expense) Coverage Form* (CP 00 30) may actually be cheaper than pure extra expense using the *Extra Expense Coverage Form* (CP 00 50). Rates to purchase the 40%-80%-100% option are two times the 80% basic property rate. Compare that rate to the Monthly Limit of Indemnity rate which, for a manufacturing operation using 1/6 monthly limit of indemnity, is only 0.95 times the 80% coinsurance basic property rate.

The insured can purchase twice as much protection, add some business income coverage on a non-coinsurance basis, and not be limited in the amount of extra expense coverage that can be used in the first 30 or 60 days. That is a much better use of the insured's premium.

Temporary (Mostly) Measures

Extra expense coverage is designed to most often cover temporary measures taken by the insured to maintain operational continuity. All such temporary measures are paid in full under the extra expense coverage.

However, some permanent measures are paid under extra expense because they do not fit the definition of "continuing normal operating expense" used in the business income policy. These permanent measures include: 1) expediting expenses for machinery and/or equipment; and 2) increased costs to speed the repair of real property.

But coverage is provided for these permanent-measure expenses only if they reduce the amount paid under the business income coverage definition. All other permanent-measure expenses are covered under business income such as operating expenses, including payroll expenses, necessary to return to full operational capability (i.e., such as overtime for employees to return the business to operational capability; see the discussion on "Loss Determination" in Chapter 3).

Chapter 12
Business Income from Dependent Properties

Insureds joined in a mutually beneficial (or even exclusively beneficial) relationship with another business entity rely on the continued operational viability of that non-related entity. Their dependence on the goods, services, or mere presence of those external businesses leaves the insured financially vulnerable to loss should the relied-upon business or entity cease to operate following a property loss, even for a short time.

Unendorsed business income coverage pays the insured's loss of income only when a covered cause of loss damages the insured location and results in a suspension of business operations. No protection is extended from the unaltered BI policy to indemnify the insured for its loss of income resulting from damage at an unrelated entity's property. The policy must be endorsed to cover this external business income exposure.

Insurance Services Office (ISO) promulgated five business income and extra expense endorsements to protect the insured from this indirect business income loss exposure.

- *Business Income from Dependent Properties - Limited International Coverage* (CP 15 01)

- *Extra Expense from Dependent Properties - Limited International Coverage* (CP 15 02)
- *Business Income from Dependent Properties - Broad Form* (CP 15 08)
- *Business Income from Dependent Propertied - Limited Form* (CP 15 09)
- *Extra Expense from Dependent Properties* (CP 15 34)

Understanding these five endorsements first requires an understanding of the four property types upon which the insured depends and which are eligible for coverage in the endorsements.

Dependent Properties Classifications

Four entity types qualify as "eligible dependent properties": 1) suppliers; 2) buyers; 3) providers; and 4) drivers. This is not ISO terminology, but such nomenclature (and rhyming) may allow for easier recall. The definition of each entity type along with their "official" names follows.

Suppliers: ISO refers to these as "Contributing Locations." Contributing locations supply the insured with the parts, materials, or services necessary to manufacture its product or provide its service.

A supplier may be the insured's sole source or main source of a critical part or service. If the contributing location cannot supply the part or service because of a property-loss-induced operational suspension, the insured cannot complete its work and is essentially out of business until the supplier resumes operations, or an alternate source for the product or service can be found.

Policy language specifies that utility service companies such as water, power, or communication services do not qualify as "supplier locations." A separate policy form outside the scope of this book covers these types of locations.

Buyers: ISO's terminology for a buyer is a "Recipient Location." A recipient location buys/accepts the products, goods or services of the insured. This may be the insured's sole buyer or one that buys a majority of the insured's output.

An example is an entity for whom the insured contractually agrees to manufacture, assemble, or provide a certain number or amount of goods or services. If the buyer's (recipient's) operations are suspended due to a covered cause of loss, it has no need to buy the insured's goods. As a result, the insured's income flow is disrupted until the recipient location returns to operational capability.

See "Business Income Insurance Could Aid Dairy Farms Caught in Cheese Squeeze" in Appendix C for a more detailed example. In the example article, one cheese producer was the sole or major buyer of milk from 88 dairy farmers in the area surrounding the cheese factory.

Providers: A provider location is a "Manufacturing Location" by ISO terminology. A manufacturing location, as used in this endorsement, is not a location owned by the insured and part of the insured's proprietary supply chain. Remember, dependent property coverage extends to protect the insured from business income losses emanating from the suspension of operations of non-related entities.

The dependent property endorsement describes a manufacturing location as one that manufactures "products for delivery to your customers under contract of sale." An example is an engineering firm that designs a piece of equipment used in the construction industry, but which does not have the facilities to manufacture the piece. Manufacturing is contracted to a specialty manufacturer. As orders for the equipment are received, the contracted manufacturing operation manufactures and assembles the finished product designed by the engineering firm.

If the manufacturing facility is damaged or destroyed by a covered cause of loss (i.e., a fire), the engineering firm loses the income from the sale of the equipment until the manufacturer returns to operational capability. The engineering firms' loss of income is covered by the dependent property form (if correctly completed).

Likewise, an independent manufacturing representative may suffer a significant loss of income if a manufacturer it represents shuts down due to a covered cause of loss and is unable to produce the product. If the insured loses income because a manufacturer can't produce the product the insured sells, there is a dependent property exposure.

Drivers: Known to ISO as a "Leader Location;" drivers can include anchor stores (Wal-Mart, Belk, Macy's, etc.), sports and entertainment venues, and other such operations or entities that draw customers to the area.

Anchor stores draw shoppers to a particular mall or shopping center. Smaller retailers depend on those stores and the shoppers they bring to the location to lure customers into their shop while on the premises. Loss of a "leader location" in the form of an anchor store can reduce the income previously enjoyed by the smaller retailer.

A less-often considered driver is a sporting or concert venue. Hotels and restaurants in the city where the Super Bowl, World Series, or other events and attractions occur generally see significant increases in the occupancy rate and customer base leading to increased income. Should the stadium be severely damaged, and the event moved, those businesses could lose a significant amount of revenue.

Consider also, casinos or other attractions that may be attached to hotels. If the casino is damaged or destroyed, the hotel is likely to lose a large amount of revenue.

What "drives" customers to the insured's location? That is the property on which the insured depends and against whose property loss the insured's income needs to be protected.

Part of the business income risk management process is uncovering these dependent property exposures. The insured may be unaware of the potential income loss created by these relationships.

Dependent Property Endorsements

Two of the five dependent property endorsements protect the insured from international exposures (if any); two focus exclusively on extra expense protection; one extends the full limit of business income (and extra expense if applicable) coverage to the dependent property; and three require the insured to specifically select a business income (and extra expense, if applicable) limit. Yes, that adds up to eight, but some crossover is present in the five forms.

Business Income from Dependent Properties - Limited International Coverage (CP 15 01): Only the dependent business income exposure created by suppliers (contributing locations) and providers (manufacturing locations) is contemplated in the CP 15 01. Additionally, the insured must select a specific amount of business income coverage to extend to those listed locations. This endorsement is designed to extend dependent property coverage for suppliers and providers located outside the traditional coverage territory (as defined in the property policy). The CP 15 01 can be used with either the CP 00 30 or the CP 00 32 and extra expense coverage can be added.

Extra Expense from Dependent Properties - Limited International Coverage (CP 15 02): This is exactly like the CP 15 01 except that the only covered exposure is the extra expense loss suffered as a result of a covered, loss-induced suspension of operations at the dependent international location. The CP 15 02 can be attached to only the pure extra expense coverage form (CP 00 50).

Business Income from Dependent Properties - Broad Form (CP 15 08): This endorsement extends business income and extra expense coverage (if the CP 00 30 is used) to dependent property losses emanating from any of the four types of dependent properties (suppliers, buyers, providers, and/or drivers). The entire business income and extra expense coverage limit is available to pay the loss resulting from the dependent property's suspension of operation, provided it is caused by a covered cause of loss.

Business Income from Dependent Properties - Limited Form (CP 15 09): Almost exactly like the CP 15 08 with one major difference, this endorsement requires the insured to specify the amount of business income (and extra expense if the CP 00 30 is attached) coverage desired. This endorsement is used if: 1) the insured did not desire business income protection at its own premises; or 2) the insured desires separate or different coverage limits for the dependent property exposure.

Extra Expense from Dependent Properties (CP 15 34): This endorsement mirrors the CP 15 09 except that only extra expenses resulting from the closure of the dependent property are covered. The endorsement can be attached to only the pure extra expense coverage form (CP 00 50). Like the CP 15 09, the insured is required to choose the limits of extra expense desired. All four dependent property types are eligible for protection under this endorsement (like the CP 15 08 and CP 15 09).

Premiums/Rates

Rates for dependent property coverage are largely based on the relationship between the insured and the dependent property when the dependent property is a supplier, buyer, or provider. If the scheduled dependent property is the sole supplier (contributing location), buyer (recipient location), or provider (manufacturing location), the rate to add this protection is double or more than double compared to the situation where there are several suppliers, buyers, or providers. The greater the dependence, the higher the rate.

Policy Provisions

Similar terms and conditions apply to all five dependent property endorsements.

1. No coverage is extended to dependent properties if the loss leading to a business shutdown is limited to damage or destruction of electronic data.
2. "Business income" and "extra expense" garner the same definitions as are found in the applicable business income or extra expense form.
3. "Period of restoration" is defined the same in the endorsements as in the policy forms.
4. The property loss to the dependent property must be from a cause that would have been covered had it happened to the insured's property. Coverage is based on the cause of loss form attached.

Both the broad and limited Business Income from Dependent Properties endorsements (the CP 15 08 and CP 15 09) stipulate that the business income loss will be reduced if the insured can resume dependent property operations by finding another buyer (recipient location) or supplier (contributing location). Further, neither the CP 15 08 or CP 15

09 can be used when the Business Income Premium Adjustment endorsement (CP 15 20) is attached.

Supply Chain Protection

Supply chain protection is not new, but the breadth of protection introduced by ISO in 2013, and available for use with all five dependent property endorsements, is. Historically the business income dependent property endorsements have extended the full limit of coverage to only those dependent properties scheduled in the endorsement. The form did include a very small amount of coverage (0.03% of the limit for each day of suspension) for properties not scheduled (aka "miscellaneous" locations described in the following section).

This limited "miscellaneous locations" coverage could be used to cover "secondary" dependent locations. A secondary dependent location is one that, for example, supplies the insured's supplier but does not have a direct business relationship with the insured. The insured's supplier cannot supply the insured if a loss to the supplier's supplier causes an operational shutdown. The insured suffers an operational shutdown because its supplier suffers an operational shutdown as a result of a business-closing loss at the supplier's supplier.

Imagine the supply chain. The insured ("A") receives widgets directly from "Supplier" ("B"). "Supplier B" needs a cog from its sub-supplier ("C") to make the widgets for "A." If "C" suffers a business-closing loss, it cannot supply "B" with the cogs that "B" needs to manufacture the widgets for "A."

This new-in-2013 optional coverage, available within all five dependent property endorsements, allows the insured

("A") to be more fully covered for its business income and/or extra expense loss due to a business-closing loss at "C's" location (the "secondary dependency").

Here are some features of this option.

- The option applies to only contributing locations ("suppliers") and recipient locations ("buyers").
- "Secondary contributing locations" and "Secondary recipient locations" are limited to direct suppliers and/or buyers of the scheduled "primary" dependent property.
- In the *Business Income from Dependent Properties – Limited International Coverage (CP 15 01)* endorsement, coverage extension to a secondary location is limited to contributing ("supplier") locations.
- Business income loss resulting from loss or damage at a secondary location is limited to the amount of business income coverage applicable to a loss that occurs at a scheduled dependent property.
- Coverage for loss at secondary locations is not additional coverage; it is part of the limit of coverage available for the listed dependent property.

Utilizing this option increases the dependent property rate by approximately 50% (rate modifications to the international form (CP 15 01) are company specific).

Additional Coverage: Miscellaneous Locations

Three dependent property endorsements extend coverage to eligible dependent properties not listed in the schedule of dependent locations. The CP 15 08, CP 15 09, and CP 15 34 provide coverage for these "miscellaneous locations."

This additional coverage extends a minimal amount of dependent property coverage for locations the insured neglected to schedule, but from which the insured suffers a dependent property loss.

Payment under this extension is limited to .03% (.0003) of the sum of all limits shown on the schedule per day of suspension. If the total scheduled dependent property limits are $1 million, the most payable under this additional coverage is $300 per day ($1,000,000 x .0003 = $300).

Look for Dependent Properties

Dependent property coverage can be a valuable coverage for the insured. As stated previously, the insured may be unaware of the exposure. Five endorsements have been created to cover nearly any dependent property exposure faced by the insured.

Chapter 13

Business Income's Miscellaneous Policy Provisions

Prior chapters detailed the main BI policy provisions and many of the external factors directly affecting the business income coverage. This chapter highlights the remaining business income policy provisions not previously discussed.

Interruption of Computer Operations - Limited Coverage

Statistically, businesses that close following a major computer malfunction are less likely to reopen than those suffering major property damage (i.e. a fire). According to the US Department of Labor, 40% of businesses suffering a catastrophic data loss never reopen. Fifty percent of the businesses that do reopen close within three years. Ninety-three percent of businesses that can't recover data within 10 days ultimately fail, according to the National Archives and Records Administration in Washington D.C.

The business income form is not designed to cover the loss of income arising out of a business closure following failure of the insured's computer system. Only a very limited amount and breadth of protection is extended to this type of business income loss.

- It covers a suspension of computer operations only if the interruption is caused by a covered cause of loss (i.e. fire). If the special cause of loss form is attached, only computer damage caused by the specified causes of loss or collapse is covered.

- The covered causes of loss are extended to include damage caused by "a virus, harmful code or similar instruction introduced into or enacted on a computer system (including electronic data) or a network to which it is connected, designed to damage or destroy any part of the system or disrupt its normal operation." No coverage is extended if the damage is caused by any employee (full-time, part-time, temporary, contract, etc.).

- Coverage is limited to $2,500 per policy year (in the aggregate).

- The coverage extension ends when the period of restoration ends. This type of loss does not extend the period of restoration.

Civil Authority

Occasions exist when, due to public safety concerns or access requirements, a civil authority evacuates businesses or individuals from a dangerous situation or area. Depending on the situational factors involved, such required evacuations and area prohibitions may last several days or weeks. The unendorsed business income coverage form extends only limited protection for such mandated business closures.

- Business income and extra expense (EE is only available if the CP 00 30 is used) is available when a property away from the insured's premises is damaged by a covered cause of loss and a civil authority (police, fire, etc.) prohibits access to the insured location.
- Damage leading to the actions of the civil authority must occur within 1 mile of the insured location.
- Business income protection begins 72 hours after the civil authority's action (unless decreased by endorsement). Extra expense coverage begins immediately upon evacuation.
- Business income and extra expense coverage is limited to four consecutive weeks.
- Civil authority coverage is not in addition to the applicable coverage limits.

This wording was revised in the 2007 version of the policy form (adopted in late 2008). Previously, the insured was granted only up to three weeks of coverage but was not subject to the 1-mile limitation. Other civil authority conditions were changed in this revision.

The business income policy can be endorsed to alter some of these limitations. Attachment of the Civil Authority Change endorsement (CP 15 32) allows the insured to modify the one-mile radius limitation and/or the four-week coverage period limit.

Alterations and New Buildings–An Automatic Additional Coverage

This 11-line provision is almost worthy of its own chapter. The alterations and new buildings additional coverage can mean the difference between an insured's successful opening or resumption of operations and the business' ultimate failure.

New Buildings or Structures: Loss of or damage to a new building or one under construction can cause the business to lose income and suffer additional expenses. This BI and EE exposure is covered by this additional coverage. Assume the insured is constructing a new store or manufacturing facility and two months prior to the date operations are slated to begin, the building burns. Rather than opening on time, the facility's opening is delayed eight months (10 months from the date of the fire). Is the insured out any income?

Yes. The insured loses the eight months of income that would have been earned had they opened as scheduled.

The eight-month income loss is covered under this additional coverage. This exposure is why it is important the insured be offered business income protection anytime a builders' risk policy is written. Remember, commercial structures exist to make money (more specifically a profit) for the owner. If the structure is not there or is delayed in opening, it cannot produce the desired income. Any delay in opening caused by a covered cause of loss leads to a loss of business income that needs to be protected against.

Alterations or Additions to Existing Buildings or Structures: This second provision essentially copies the first except it relates to work on existing buildings. If a covered cause of loss delays the planned opening and operation of the altered or renovated structure, this part pays for the resulting loss of business income.

Machinery, Equipment, Supplies, or Building Materials: If damage to or destruction of any machinery, equipment, supplies, or building materials delays the opening and operation of the building, the resulting loss of income is covered under this additional coverage's third provision. For example, if all the floor tiles are damaged, destroyed or stolen while on the job site, any delay in opening caused by such loss or damage is covered by this section.

A scenario more likely than the stolen tile is the damage to or destruction of a machine critical to a manufacturing operation before it is installed. This particular example machine is custom-made and requires six months to build. Two weeks before opening, a fire runs through the building and destroys the machine. The building is not badly damaged and can be repaired within the remaining two-week period, but the machine is destroyed and must be replaced. Because the machine is required for the manufacturing process, the operation cannot open until it is replaced. The six-month loss of income is covered by this policy provision.

How This Section Works: Business income limits, like all property limits, are provided on a per-loss basis, that is, the limits are reinstated in preparation for a second (or even third) covered loss. The loss of business income under this provision is calculated from the day the operation should have begun had no loss occurred and ends when operations should reasonably be expected to begin.

Just because operations have not begun does not mean that income can't be lost.

Newly Acquired Locations

Business income (and extra expense coverage if using the CP 00 30) can be extended to apply to newly acquired locations. But just like other property coverage forms, there are limitations.

1. Business income coverage must be provided on a coinsurance basis (not available with a non-coinsurance option).
2. The maximum amount payable under this extension is $100,000 at any newly acquired location.
3. Coverage is limited to a maximum of 30 days.

The coinsurance condition does not apply to locations covered under this extension.

Chapter 14
Details of Time Element's Endorsements

Many business income-specific endorsements were discussed in prior chapters as shown below. This chapter briefly describes the business income and extra expense endorsements not previously detailed.

Business Income from Dependent Properties – Limited International Coverage (CP 15 01): See Chapter 12

Extra Expense from Dependent Properties – Limited International Coverage (CP 15 02): See Chapter 12

Business Income – Landlord as Additional Insured (Rental Value) (CP 15 03): Lease agreements often require tenants to provide business income protection for the benefit of the landlord covering his/her potential loss of rents following a covered cause of loss. The CP 15 03 was created as a means to meet this requirement. It is available for use with both Business Income coverage forms (CP 00 30 and CP 00 32). Use of this endorsement allows the tenant to cover its own business income exposure plus the landlord's loss-of-rents exposure to satisfy the contract (since ongoing rents is considered a continuing normal operating expense when required by contract). The insured chooses Business Income Including Loss of Rents or Rental Value only (if not covering its own business income exposure).

Discretionary Payroll Expense (CP 15 04): Available for use with both business income forms (CP 00 30 and CP 00 32), this endorsement (made available in 2008) allows the insured to cover the payroll expenses of specified individuals or classes of employees whose services are not necessary to resume operations. Coverage can be provided for the entire period of restoration (POR) or a set number of days (the days do not have to be sequential).

Business income coverage forms specify that a part of the BI loss includes the payroll expenses of employees "...necessary to resume operations." An employee may not be necessary to the resumption of the operations, but the insured may still want to cover that employee's payroll for economic or any other reason it chooses. Payroll of an employee not necessary for the resumption of the operation is considered discretionary.

Apparently, this endorsement was created due to a misunderstanding or misapplication of the business income form. Payroll expenses are not excluded in the unendorsed business income form unless the Payroll Limitation or Exclusion endorsement (CP 15 10). (See "Loss Determination" in Chapter 3.)

Food Contamination (Business Interruption and Extra Expense) (CP 15 05): This endorsement allows insureds the option to purchase coverage to protect against business income and/or extra expense losses resulting from food contamination. Key provisions of this endorsement include the following.

- Coverage is triggered when: 1) the insured is ordered closed by the applicable governmental authority (i.e. the board of health); and 2) the closure is the result of the discovery of or suspicion of "food contamination."

- "Food contamination" means: An outbreak of food poisoning or food-related illness arising out of: 1) tainted food distributed or purchased by the insured; 2) food improperly processed, stored, handled or prepared by the insured; or 3) food contaminated by virus or bacteria transmitted by one or more employees of the insured.

- The policy pays: 1) the insured's expense to clean equipment (as required by the governmental authority); 2) the cost to replace food actually or suspected to be contaminated; 3) the costs of employee medical tests and vaccinations (this does not pay what would be paid by workers' compensation; 4) the loss of business income beginning 24 hours after the insured receives the notice of closure; and 5) additional advertising expenses incurred to restore the insured's reputation.

- A specific limit is chosen and entered into the endorsement. This limit is an annual aggregate limit. A separate limit is required for advertising expense if the coverage is desired.

- The policy does not cover the costs of fines or penalties imposed by the regulatory authority (these are business risk expenses).

Expanded Limits on Loss Payment (CP 15 07): See Chapter 11.

Business Income from Dependent Properties – Broad Form (CP 15 08): See Chapter 12.

Business Income from Dependent Properties – Limited Form (CP 15 09): See Chapter 12.

Payroll Limitation or Exclusion (CP 15 10): See Chapter 4.

Power, Heat & Refrigeration Deduction (CP 15 11): See Chapter 4.

Seasonal Limits – Monthly Limits on Loss Payment (CP 15 13): Insureds who rent space on a seasonal basis may not have a need for 12 months of business income protection at those locations. Examples include specialty Christmas shops (open from about September through December) or seasonal gift shops (the shop's location influences the season it is open). All operational income is earned during these brief seasons, so coverage is only necessary during those seasons. Limits of coverage are specified on a monthly basis and only paid during the months scheduled and in the amounts listed. The endorsement cannot be attached to the Extra Expense coverage form. To correctly activate coverage, 100% coinsurance must be indicated on the declarations page and there must be a written lease.

Business Income Report/Worksheet (CP 15 15): Referenced throughout the book; most specifically in chapters 2, 3, 4, 5, and 6.

Business Income Premium Adjustment (CP 15 20): See Chapter 7.

Mining Properties – Business Income (CP 15 24): As the name suggests, this endorsement customizes the business income policy to allow it to meet the unique needs of mining properties. The endorsement allows the insured to choose one of three options (none, limited or broad) to dictate how the business income coverage applies when underground property is damaged. Additionally, finished stock is redefined to include materials that have been mined or processed because the period of restoration does not include the time required to replace finished stock.

Business Income Changes – Educational Institutions (CP 15 25): Schools require special treatment regarding business income protection. This endorsement changes the definition of the period of restoration, making it a function of the beginning of the academic term immediately following the ability of the school to return to operational capability, rather than limiting it to the day the insured is able to return to operation. The extended business income protection is also a function of the beginning of the academic term. Income derived from bookstores, athletic events, research grants or any activity other than those that generate tuition is excluded from the definition of business income. To qualify, coverage must be written on a coinsurance basis using at least 50% coinsurance. Additionally, each school term must be described on an annual basis.

Electronic Media and Records (CP 15 29): Revises the electronic media and records loss condition. The limitation can be removed or the number of days of coverage can be increased beyond the 60 given in the unendorsed business income form.

Ordinance or Law – Increased Period of Restoration (CP 15 31): See Chapter 5.

Civil Authority Changes (CP 15 32): The unendorsed time element forms limit coverage for business income lost or extra expense incurred as a direct result of the actions of a civil authority (fire, police, etc.) to only four consecutive weeks and only if the damage leading to such action occurs within a one-mile radius of the insured's premises. The endorsement allows the insured to modify the one-mile and/or four-week limitations contained in all three forms (CP 00 30, CP 00 32, and CP 00 50).

Individual risk characteristics must be examined to determine if the endorsement is needed by a particular insured. Examples of situations that may require this extension include an insured being in close proximity to a chemical plant or other facility that may cause the civil authority to evacuate an area wider than a mile or for more than four weeks, or the insured's exposure to some sort of natural disaster (wildfires, hurricanes, etc.) that may keep it away for more than four weeks.

Extra Expense from Dependent Properties (CP 15 34): See Chapter 12.

Utility Services – Time Element (CP 15 45): A suspension of operations leading to a business income loss caused solely by an interruption of a supplied utility (water, waste water removal, communications, or power) is excluded in the unendorsed business income policy. This endorsement removes that exclusion, extending business income and extra expense protection if the supply from the chosen utility is interrupted. The endorsement even allows the insured the option of extending coverage to overhead transmission lines for both communication and power supply for an additional premium.

A separate limit of coverage must be chosen to cover the suspension of operations caused by disruption of the covered utility service(s). The loss does not fall under the policy's business income or extra expense limit, but neither does the coinsurance condition apply to the coverage provided by this endorsement.

Radio or Television Antennas – Business Income or Extra Expense (CP 15 50): This endorsement changes the cause of loss coverage form rather than the business income forms by removing the radio and television antenna exclusion. Business income lost due to a suspension of operations resulting from or caused by damage to a radio or television antenna is covered when this endorsement is attached.

Business Income Changes – Beginning of the Period of Restoration (CP 15 56): Allows the insured to eliminate the 72-hour waiting period by reducing it to 24 hours or down to no waiting period. The 2008 revision of this endorsement resulted in the withdrawal of the CP 15 55 (Business Income Changes – Time Period).

Business Income and/or Extra Expense Coverage for Year 2000 Computer-Related And Other Electronic Problems (CP 15 57): As the name suggests, should a year 2000 computer problem cause a business suspension, only a limited amount of business income or extra expense protection is provided.

ISO was contacted regarding the future of this endorsement and said, *"ISO has no plans to sunset this endorsement at this time. While the Year 2000 was the impetus for the endorsement, it [the CP 15 57] applies more generally to the inability of systems to identify dates from the year 2000 and beyond. This endorsement specifies that certain risks associated with computer or other electronic equipment failure, malfunction and inadequacy — or inabilities to correctly recognize, process, distinguish, interpret or accept one or more dates or times — are excluded from coverage."*

Appendix A

Step-by-Step Instructions for Completing the Business Income Application

Understanding business income protection does little good if the information cannot be translated to the underwriter via the application. The ACORD 810 is the industry-standard application used to provide the insurance carrier with all the information necessary to deliver the proper business income and/or extra expense program. While some carriers use proprietary forms, this chapter focuses on ACORD's forms.

Each section is individually described to assure that the proper information is provided. Some data requested on this form is antiquated and does not apply to the current BI coverage forms. However, the questions have yet to be removed from the application.

ACORD 140 - The Property Application

Understanding the steps necessary to indicate the desire for business income and or extra expense protection in the Property Application (ACORD 140) is required before moving to the supplemental application (ACORD 810). Nine questions must be answered in the ACORD 140 none of which are specific to business income and extra expense coverage.

SUBJECT OF INSURANCE: Three options related to business income (BI) and/or extra expense (EE) are available for entry here.

- ***BI w/EE*** to indicate the insured's desire to purchase business income and extra expense protection prompting the underwriter to use the CP 00 30. The definition of BI is more thoroughly defined in the supplemental application.
- ***BI*** indicates that the insured wants business income coverage only. The underwriter should know from this that the CP 00 32 is desired.
- ***EE*** tells the underwriter that pure extra expense coverage is desired leading them to attach the CP 00 50 Extra Expense Coverage Form.

AMOUNT: The desired coverage amount is input here. This can be the amount found on Line "L" of the CP 15 15 (the total of the BI exposure on Line J, the EE amount in Line K.1., and the Extended Business Income amount in K.2.) multiplied by the chosen coinsurance percentage; or it could be the guesstimate amount chosen by an insured using either the Monthly Limit of Indemnity or the Maximum Period of Indemnity options.

COINS %: Only applies when the insured is using the unaltered coverage form or the Business Income Agreed Amount option. The applicable percentage (50-125%) is entered.

VALUATION: This can be left blank as it does not necessarily apply to time element coverage. If the insured is using the coinsurance option, ALS (meaning actual loss sustained) could be input; however, that might just cause confusion. It's best just left blank.

CAUSES OF LOSS: Same as the property coverage forms.

INFLATION GUARD %: Does not apply to BI coverage.

DED: Use the applicable number of hours. 72 hours is the standard time deductible unless lowered using the CP 15 56. If lowered, enter the correct number of hours (24 or 0).

BLKT #: Use as necessary.

ADDITIONAL INFORMATION: Remember to check the *BUSINESS INCOME/EXTRA EXPENSE* box pointing the underwriter to the ACORD 810.

ACORD 810 – Supplemental Application

PREMISES INFORMATION: Information must be provided on a location-specific or blanket basis.

   Coverage Desired: Two of five blocks next to the premises' information may need to be checked, unless the insured only wants extra expense protection or doesn't desire coverage for the loss of rents. One of the first three blocks must be checked, and the remaining two are optional based on the coverage desired.

- **Business Income / Extra Expense**: Check this block if the insured wants both BI and EE. Just like the information provided under Subject of Insurance, marking this box alerts the underwriter to attach the CP 00 30.

- **Business Income w/o Extra Expense**: Alerts the underwriter that only BI coverage is desired and leads the underwriter to attach the CP 00 32.

- **Extra Expense**: Used when the insured wants only EE protection. The underwriter knows to use the CP 00 50.

If either of the two business income options is checked (with or without extra expense), one of the two remaining blocks regarding rental value may also need to be checked. If no rental value coverage is desired, these can be left blank.

- **Business Income/Rental Value**: This box is checked if the insured needs to cover rental value as part of the total business income coverage.

- **Rental Value**: Checking this box indicates that the insured only wants rental value coverage. If this box is checked, no income other than loss of rents is protected.

TYPE OF BUSINESS: Rather self-explanatory. Simply choose whether the insured is a non-manufacturing entity (NON MFG), a manufacturing operation (MFG) or a MINING operation. Indicating the business type aids the insured in knowing which parts of the business income report/worksheet to complete and clues the underwriter to specific endorsements required.

This block is also the place to indicate the chosen coinsurance percentage by filling in the blank next to **% COINS**.

ORDINARY PAYROLL: There are two main options under ordinary payroll: 1) Excluded (EXCL); and 2) Included (INCL) (the default setting in the BI form). If Excluded (EXCL) is checked, the underwriter knows to attach the CP 15 10 and the insured must deduct excluded payroll from Total Revenues (Line H) in the business income worksheet.

Checking EXCL also requires the insured to stipulate how long payroll is provided to otherwise excluded employees. There are two options presented: 90 days and 180 days. There are also two blank lines allowing the insured to make other choices. One allows a number of days of coverage (i.e. none or 60) and the second indicates/allows an amount of payroll to be excluded; but the revised rules may not allow for these options to be used.

The ACORD application has not yet been updated to correspond with the 2013 CP 15 10 endorsement changes (see Chapter 4 for more detail). Until the application is updated, if "EXCL" is checked, specify in the description WHICH employees are excluded (remember, there are four options).

EXT PERIOD: Should the insured desire extended business income coverage beyond the automatic 60 days provided by the policy's Extended Business Income provision, this box is checked and the desired number of days of additional coverage is indicated. The amount of additional coverage should already be indicated on Line K.2 of the CP 15 15.

MO PERIOD: This box is checked if the insured wants the Monthly Limit of Indemnity non-coinsurance option. In the block the desired limit of coverage is indicated. Indicate the desired percentage (1/3, 1/4, or 1/6) in the OTHER COVERAGES section by referencing MO PERIOD.

MAX PERIOD: The second non-indemnity, non-coinsurance option is Maximum Period of Indemnity. If the insured desires this option, simply check the block and indicate the limit of coverage. There is no need to do anything else because the policy already limits coverage to 120 days.

POWER/HEAT: Checking this block is only necessary if the insured can deduct the cost of power or heat by contract. The amount of the deduction (DED) is found in the CP 15 15 as a deducted, non-continuing production-related expense. Checking this block prompts the underwriter to attach the CP 15 11.

ELEC MEDIA: This block in NO LONGER necessary. It is a holdover from the 1995 and earlier editions of the business income forms when coverage for electronic media was limited to 60 days. This coverage is now subject to an aggregate limit of coverage.

ORD OR LAW: Check this block if the insured needs Ordinance or Law coverage. The underwriter attaches the CP 15 31 when this box is checked. DO NOT choose a number of days; this is not necessary. The endorsement states that the policy will include any increase in rebuilding time due to the application of a building code as part of the period of restoration. The request for a number of days must be a holdover from an old edition of the endorsement but is not necessary now.

CIVIL AUTH: If the insured needs to extend the coverage for actions by a civil authority beyond the four weeks or 1 mile parameters provided in the policy, this box is checked. Within the block there is room only to increase the number of days; there is no space to change the mileage limitation. To change the mileage parameters to something greater than 1 mile, use the OTHER COVERAGES section. The underwriter should attach the CP 15 32 if this box is checked and indicate the desired changes.

OFF PREM POWER: The terminology is antiquated but the intent is the same; this block would probably be better termed OFF PREM UTILITY as this is the block checked if the insured desires to extend business income protection to cover losses resulting from an interruption of one of the subject utilities: 1) POWER; 2) WATER; or 3) Communications (COMM). There is no place to indicate whether the insured wants to include coverage for damage to overhead lines (power or communications) or not. Simply place this information in the OTHER COVERAGES section. The off-premises utility must be described in the box between the top section and the OTHER COVERAGES section entitled, "NAME(S) AND ADDRESSES FOR OFF PREM POWER OF DEPEND PROP." The CP 15 45 should be attached when this block is checked.

TUITION FEES: This part only applies if the insured is a school. The definition of business income is changed to include as business income only student tuitions and other student-related educational income (i.e. room and board). Educational institutions do not include in the definition of business income any income derived from bookstores, athletic events, research grants or any activity other than those which generate tuition or other student-related fees. Checking this box prompts the underwriter to attach the CP 15 25 endorsement.

DEPEND PROP: This box is checked if the insured is extending business income coverage to apply when there is damage to Dependent Properties. The insured indicates which of the five dependent property forms is being used by checking one of the next three boxes. The options are the BROAD FORM (CP 15 08), LIMITED FORM (CP 15 09) or a blank where one of the other three available forms can be manually entered (see Chapter 12 for details).

The **COIN** _____ % line within the DEPEND PROP section is where the agent indicates the coinsurance applicable to the policy as a whole. This is the same percentage as that listed in the TYPE OF BUSINESS block. This line does not really appear to be necessary as none of the dependent property forms reference coinsurance. Four of the forms require the insured to pick a specific limit for this coverage extension. Only the CP 15 08 Broad Form extends the full amount of business income protection to any loss caused by a dependent property, so there does not appear to be any need for the percentage.

Although dependent property limits must be specifically chosen and listed in four of the five forms, there is no place in this block to enter that information. Use the OTHER COVERAGES section to detail these limits.

Finally, the DEPEND PROP section requires the type of dependent property be indicated by checking one of four blocks.

1. CONT LOC is Contributing Location (Supplier).
2. REC LOC is a Recipient Location (Buyer).
3. MFG LOC is a Manufacturing Location (Provider).
4. LDR LOC is a Leader Location (Driver).

Describe each dependent property in the section between the top and the OTHER COVERAGES sections entitled, "NAME(S) AND ADDRESSES FOR OFF PREM POWER OF DEPEND PROP."

EXTRA EXPENSE: This is the last section of the supplemental application and applies only if "pure" extra expense coverage is written (using the CP 00 50). As per the extra expense commentary, the extra expense limit is paid out based on the percentages chosen. In this block, the chosen percentages are entered in the blanks provided under LIMIT

LOSS PAY. Generally, three blanks will be used; only when the CP 15 07 is attached will the fourth percentage blank be filled.

A second piece of information requested in this block is the estimated period of restoration (_____ **DAYS PERIOD REST**). There is NO need for this information as coverage is not limited to a specific number of days. The only two limitations applying to extra expense coverage are the 30-day percentages (as indicated above and in Chapter 11) and the total coverage limit purchased by the insured. Nothing in the form limits the coverage to a specific number of days, so ignore this block.

Appendix B
Business Income Insurance & Risk Management Checklist

Risk Management /Coverage Question	Y	N	Notes
Type of Operation (Mfg., Non-Mfg.; Mining)[1]			
Has the Business Income Report/Worksheet been completed for the **UPCOMING** year? [2]			
Does the insured's business income fluctuate erratically making estimation difficult?[3]			
Is "**payroll**" limited by attachment of the CP 15 10? • For which employees? • For what amount of time?			
Any specific employee's services required for the business return to operational capability? [4]			
Can the insured contractually reduce/cut any part of the utility services following a loss? • How much? • Has the CP 15 11 been attached?			
How quickly can production machinery be replaced?			
Is the building in full compliance with all current building codes? [5]			
Does the insured's BI limit include "rental income" from the insured location?			
Can the insured operate from an alternative location? [6]			
Are the products or services offered by the insured "on-going;" requiring the insured to be operational very quickly? [7]			
Have the following been estimated (a worksheet is available)? [8] • The "period of restoration" • The coinsurance percentage • The business income limit			
Does the insured rely on any other properties or entities for a major source of income? (Suppliers, Buyers, Providers or Drivers)			
Has the insured chosen to apply Agreed Value Protection? • Has the CP 15 15 been completed? • What coinsurance percentage is being applied?			
Has the insured chosen to use the Monthly Limit of Indemnity option? • What is the BI limit? • What is the Extra Expense Limit? • What fraction is being used? [9]			

• Is the Maximum Period of Indemnity option being used? • What is the limit of coverage?		
• Is the insured's business seasonal? (10)		

(1) Three options: Manufacturing; Non-manufacturing, or Mining.

(2) Remember, business income coinsurance calculations are based on information for the policy period, not the information for the prior 12 months. This is an estimate but required.

(3) If the insured's business income fluctuates greatly from year to year, consider attaching the Business Income Premium Adjustment endorsement (CP 15 20). It makes the form a reporting/auditable form assuring the insured pays the correct premium from year to year.

(4) If the services of a specific employee are required to return the business to operational capability or the employee has special skills and talents, that employee should be listed as an exception on the CP 15 10 limiting endorsement.

(5) If the building is not in compliance, the time to rebuild the structure may be increased. This additional time must be taken into account when estimating the period of restoration. Consider attaching the CP 15 31 and increasing the business income limits.

(6) If the insured can operate from an alternate location, only a small amount of business income may be required. Extra Expense may be the more necessary coverage. It may be better to provide extra expense using the CP 00 30 as the rate per $100 is lower.

(7) Newspapers, banks, insurance agencies, etc. must be open very quickly. Extra Expenses are these operations greatest exposure.

(8) Use the calculator provided in Chapter 7.

(9) Three options: 1/3, 1/4 and 1/6.

(10) Attach the Seasonal Limits endorsement (CP 15 13) and specifically schedule the monthly income amounts.

Appendix C

Business Income Insurance Could Aid Dairy Farms Caught in Cheese Squeeze

Who would have thought that a cheese factory's inability to make mozzarella cheese would cost so many dairy farmers their livelihood? Eighty-eight (88) dairy farmers in western Vermont and New York took an economic hit from a September 29 (2008) fire at the Saputo Cheese USA plant in Hinesburg, Vt. (about 12 miles southeast of Burlington).

News reports quoted Vermont's Department of Agriculture Food and Markets as saying that the cheese plant purchased nearly 1 million pounds of milk per day, which totaled 10% to 12% of the state's entire milk production. Each of the 88 dairy farmers, on average, supplied the plant with more than 11,300 pounds of milk every day. Unless alternate buyers could be found, the farmers would lose this major source of income for at least another two months, according to company officials.

The dairy farmers' loss of income arising out of the fire damage to Saputo could have been covered under the dairies' business income policies, if they had them. Attaching one of the two "dependent properties" endorsements would have provided the necessary protection against this loss of income.

- Business Income From Dependent Properties - Broad Form (CP 15 08)

- Business Income From Dependent Properties - Limited
  Form (CP 15 09)

The two forms offer the same breadth of coverage; the limit
of business income coverage is the only difference. The Broad
Form (CP 15 08) makes the entire business income limit
available to cover a dependent property loss; whereas the
Limited Form (CP 15 09) allows the insured to choose lower
coverage limits applicable to dependent property loses or
provide dependent property coverage without purchasing
business income for the insured location.

Four classes of dependent properties are extended
coverage under these endorsements.

- Contributing locations – Those that supply the insured
  with materials and products.
- Recipient locations – Those the buy from the insured.
- Manufacturing locations – Those that are within the
  insured's manufacturing chain (also an insured).
- Leader locations – Those that draw customers to the
  location of the insured.

Saputo Cheese is a recipient location for each of the dairy
farmers and likely accounted for a large percentage of the
farmers' annual income. Losing a large part of its income for
three months could be devastating for any insured. However,
there is an insurance solution to this exposure.

Few businesses fail following a major loss due to the lack of
property coverage. Most business that don't reopen or that

close shortly after reopening do so because of the devastating loss of income. Insuring the possibility of business income loss arising out of direct damage and the loss of income resulting from damage to or destruction of a dependent property could save the insured from financial ruin.

(From an Oct. 21, 2008, article on
www.MyNewMarkets.com)

Appendix D
Business Income Gaps of the BOP

Business income protection provided by the Businessowners Policy (BOP) is relationally broad; there is no coinsurance with which the agent or insured need be concerned, and the loss of income is "fully" covered for 12 months (actual loss sustained). But even in its breadth three weaknesses exist.

1. Ordinary payroll is limited to 60 days.
2. Coverage is limited to 12 months of protection.
3. Extended business income is limited to 60 days.

Ordinary Payroll Limitation

Ordinary payroll is not limited in the standard business income policies unless done so by endorsement. The BOP is exactly opposite. Unless endorsed otherwise, coverage for ordinary payroll is limited to 60 days. Should the insured desire to extend payroll to ordinary employees beyond the 60 days, the insured must; 1) endorse the policy by notating on the declaration page indicating the number of days coverage is desired; and 2) pay additional premium.

"Ordinary" employees are all employees other than officers, executives, department managers, employees under contract, or any other employees specifically listed as being necessary, non-ordinary employees (done by name or job classification). Payroll for these non-ordinary employees is covered for the entire period of restoration or 12 months, whichever comes first.

Note: ISO changed the CP 15 10 in 2013, removing the concept of "ordinary payroll." Ordinary payroll is no longer a consideration in the standard business income policy, now the insured has the option to limit or remove the payroll of any individual or group of employees. With this change, the business income coverage provided by the BOP becomes even more restrictive than the standard business income coverage.

Period of Restoration Limitation

Should the period of restoration extend beyond the 12 months of coverage provided by the standard BOP's business income protection, the insured has no remedy. Business income lost after the allowable 12-month period of indemnity is paid out of the insured's pocket.

Many factors directly affect the period of restoration and the time it takes a particular entity to return to its pre-loss operational capability. Among the relevant factors: time for the adjustment process; time for building plans to be drawn and approved; finding and hiring a contractor; obtaining building permits; time to rebuild; and any building code-related issues.

Depending on the loss severity and problems in accomplishing all the necessary period of restoration factors, the insured may require more than 12 months to return to operational capability. The BOP offers no way for the insured to increase the protection beyond 12 months. Some carriers now offer 18 months of business income coverage in their proprietary BOPs.

 Operational capability as it relates to business income is an entity's ability to operate at or near pre-loss production or sales capacity. This is a non-policy-defined business income term describing the point at which an insured can operate with the same level of inventory, equipment and efficiency as before the operational-closing loss.

To clarify, operational capability is NOT synonymous with a return to pre-loss income levels, which may take much longer to accomplish. It is merely the entity's ability to produce goods and provide service at the same level, efficiency and speed as before the loss (i.e. the ability to conduct operations at pre-loss levels). This highlights the third limitation of the BOP's business income coverage; the 60-day limit on the extended period of indemnity.

Extended Business Income Limitation

Once the business has reopened and returned to full operational capability, returning to pre-loss cash flows and income levels may take a while. The unendorsed/unaltered BOP provides only 60 days of additional protection following the period of restoration to return to pre-loss profit levels. If the insured feels this is an inadequate limit (which it probably is), the period of extended business income coverage can be extended by a notation on the declaration page and the payment of an additional premium.

Appendix E
Glossary of Terms

Accrual Basis of Accounting

Per the IRS: Under an accrual method of accounting, income is reported in the year it is earned and expenses are deducted or capitalized in the year incurred. The purpose of an accrual method of accounting is to match income and expenses in the correct year.

All Normal Operating Expenses (ANOE)

Operating expenses that would have been incurred had no business-closing loss occurred.

Amount Subject to Loss

Maximum Coinsurance Percentage **x** 12 months business income calculation (J.1 or J.2 amount)

Business Income

Net profit or loss before taxes that would have been earned had no loss occurred PLUS continuing normal operating expenses.

Compensable Business Income

The actual amount of business income paid during the period of restoration; the amount necessary to indemnify the insured. May be less than the insurable business income because it is based on net profit or loss plus actual on-going (continuing) expenses incurred during the period of restoration.

Continuing (Normal) Operating Expenses

Normal, usual, or customary operating expenditures that continue (in whole or in part) during the time the operations are discontinued (the Period of Restoration) due to a direct property loss.

Contributing Location

A dependent property location that supplies the insured with the parts, materials or services necessary to manufacture its product or provide its service. (aka suppliers)

Discretionary Payroll

Payroll expenses of specified individuals or classes of employees whose services are not necessary to resume operations. Created by an endorsement that seems unnecessary.

Dual Purpose Operation

Operations that receive income from both manufacturing and non-manufacturing operations which are not directly relatable to the manufacturing process.

Extra Expense

Necessary additional expenses that would not have been incurred had no direct property damage occurred.

Gap Factor

An increase in limit over the amount of the developed business income exposure to account for any unexpected increase in revenue and/or to provide a cushion against any unexpected extension in the period of restoration.

Insurable Business Income

The amount of business income used to calculate the business income premium; the J.1 total. This amount includes all of an entity's operating expenses with the exception of a few non-continuing sales-related and production-related expenses to arrive at the insurable business income amount. Whether these other expenses continue, are reduced or disappear during the period of restoration doesn't matter.

Jurisdictional Authority Rule

States using this as the measure of major damage allow the authority having jurisdiction (the local government) to decide when a damaged building must be brought into compliance with the current building code.

Leader Location
These can include anchor stores, sports and entertainment venues and other such operations or entities that draw customers to the area or drive them to the insured location. (aka drivers)

Major Damage
The amount of damage required for the jurisdictional authority to require the structure be brought into compliance with the current building code. See Jurisdictional Authority Rule and Percentage Rule.

Manufacturing Location
A dependent property location that manufactures products for delivery to your customers under contract of sale. (aka Provider)

Maximum Coinsurance Percentage
Number of months required to accomplish the four period of restoration objectives / 12 (the number of months in a year)

Net Income
In the context of business income, "net income" means the entity's net profit (or loss) before the application of income taxes. In practicality, the BI meaning of net income can be best explained to the accountant as real and potential earnings before taxes (EBT).

Operational Capability

An entity's ability to operate at or near pre-loss production or sales capacity. This is a non-policy business income term describing the point at which a manufacturing operation can return to pre-loss production levels and inventory levels (excluding the recreation of finished stock); and a non-manufacturing entity can operate with the same level of inventory, equipment and efficiency as before the operational-closing loss.

Operational Continuity

The ability of the business to continue to operate and produce some amount of goods or services following a loss-induced business suspension.

Ordinary Employee

These are employees not classified as officers, executives, department managers, employees under contract, or any specifically listed employee or job description. This definition applies to only the BOP coverage form following revisions to the CP 15 10 in 2013.

Ordinary Payroll

Payroll of ordinary employees. This definition applies to only the BOP coverage form following revisions to the CP 15 10 in 2013.

Percentage Rule

States and jurisdictions applying this rule require a building damaged beyond a certain percentage of its value be brought, in its entirety, into compliance with local building code.

Period of Restoration

The period of time that begins after the direct physical loss or damage by a Covered Cause of Loss at the described premises (a time deductible applies and differs based on the coverage (BI or EE); and ends on the earlier of: (1) The date when the property at the described premises should be repaired, rebuilt or replaced with reasonable speed and similar quality; or (2) the date when business is resumed at a new permanent location.

Pre-Construction Duties

Development and approval of the new building plans; advertising for, interviewing and selecting a general contractor; applying for and waiting on building permits; and scheduling and completing site clearance work.

Pre-Loss Operational Income

The ability to generate revenues at the same level enjoyed prior to the suspension of operations.

Production-Related Expenses

Cost of goods sold (COGS); outside services resold; utility services that do not continue under contract; specified payroll; and special deductions for mining operations.

Recipient Location

A dependent property location that buys/accepts the products, goods or services of the insured. (aka Buyer)

Rolling Total

Relates to pure extra expense coverage provided in the CP 00 50 (Extra Expense Coverage Form). The insured chooses a rolling total payout percentage, meaning that the insured has access to progressively higher percentages of the total limit during each 30-day period.

Sales-Related Expenses

Pre-paid outgoing freight, returns and allowances and discounts as costs associated with the post-production sales process. Bad debt that cannot be collected from buyers of the insured's product.

Collection expenses that reduce the amount of cash available to cover business-related expenses and generate a profit.

Time Doctrine

All business income losses are settled based on the coverage limit purchased. An accurate business income coverage limit calculation depends on an accurate estimation of: 1) the 12-month business income exposure; and 2) the legitimate estimation of the worst-case period of restoration. Estimating the worst-case period of restoration necessitates understanding the time required to accomplish each of the 10 steps in the four period of restoration objectives. The key to business income is the correct estimation of time.

Author Biography

Christopher J. Boggs is the Executive Director of the Big I Virtual University. He joined the insurance industry in 1990 and is a self-proclaimed insurance geek with a true passion for the insurance profession and a desire for continual learning.

During his career, Boggs has authored hundreds of insurance and risk management-related articles on a wide range of topics as diverse as Credit Default Swaps, the MCS-90, and enterprise risk management.

Boggs other insurance and risk management books include:

- *"The Insurance Professional's Practical Guide to Workers' Compensation: From History through Audit – Second Edition"*
- *"Property and Casualty Insurance Concepts Simplified: The Ultimate 'How to' Insurance Guide for Agents, Brokers, Underwriters and Adjusters"*
- *"Wow! I Never Knew That! 12 of the Most Misunderstood and Misused P&C Coverages, Concepts and Exclusions"*
- *"Insurance, Risk & Risk Management! The Insurance Professional's Guide to Risk Management and Insurance"*

A graduate of Liberty University with a bachelor's degree in Journalism, Boggs has continually pursued career-related education, obtaining nine professional insurance designations.

- Chartered Property Casualty Underwriter (**CPCU**)
- Associate in Risk Management (**ARM**)

- Associate in Loss Control Management (**ALCM**)
- Legal Principles Claims Management (**LPCS**)
- Accredited Advisor in Insurance (**AAI**)
- Associate in Premium Auditing (**APA**)
- Certified Workers' Compensation Advisor (**CWCA**)
- Construction Risk and Insurance Specialist (**CRIS**)
- Associate in General Insurance (**AINS**)

Made in the USA
Columbia, SC
24 November 2023

27075148R00117